Francesco Gamba

PSYCANTHROPY

The circle of life

A 4D projection of the brief story of a human being from its arrival in the world to its departure.

ISBN: 978-1533068095

Wherever he lives, a man exists inasmuch as he is a member of a social group, as small as it is.

Peter Farb

Primitive man was faced with the alternative of marrying out and being killed out.

E. B. Taylor

Preface

To find a title for a book of scientific divulgation is not an easy thing. At the beginning, I thought of entitling it "Handbook of Anthropological Psychology" but the word "handbook" seemed to recall those booklets that once you brought with you at the State certification exam to fix the memory gaps, full of idle notions disconnected from each other. The term "treatise" could seem too serious instead; that's why I finally decided to appeal the readers' curiosity and use the acronym Psycanthropy as title. It doesn't refer to any mysterious lunar pathology but it puts together the two main dimensions of the four ones to which the subheading outlines: psychology and cultural anthropology. The other two dimensions, as I will explain later, are genetics and ethology.

Evolutionism and genetics, that descends from the former, help us understand everything that is innate in us and has been inherited by biological way, until now considered immutable; while anthropology, through the observation and the study of the different groups of beings organized into societies, in brief of all the human groups that inhabit or inhabited the Earth, help us to understand everything that is inherited by cultural way. We mean by culture everything that is man's work, from the material production such as canoe or plough (artifacts) to the immaterial one such as languages, myths and religions. Myths are linguistic constructions provided with a meaning collectively shared that, through stories, tales and narra-

4

tions try to give a sense to what appears nonsensical in the experience of the human life, such as the existence itself; birth, illness, death, anticipating the scientific thought but using its own speculative method. The majority of the anthropologists assign to myths, and to religions, the value of well-founded elements of the material and social reality in which the human group, that produced them, operates. For this purpose, we need cosmogonic myths, in relation to the creation of the universe, or to the creation of man and all living species.

The evolutionary biologist R. Dawkins coined the term "memes", analogous and assonant to "genes", to take into account the method of transmission of the cultural elements through generations, analogous to the genetic transmission by biological way that characterized the human evolution.

Lastly, the ethology, risen in the 1930s, studies animal behavior. The imprinting phenomenon, discovered by Konrad Lorentz on ducks and the successive studies on primate, and especially on anthropomorphic apes, influenced enormously the psychology, anticipating by a few years what the genetics researchers effectively proved later on: whether we like it or not, we are closely related to our gorilla and chimpanzee cousins, especially to the Bonobos, dwarf chimpanzees first "discovered" and studied by the ethologist Frans de Waal.

All the human beings, since the origin of the first civilizations, meaning by civilizations social groups provided with structure and organization, used their mind capabilities to give meaning to natural phenomenons, as they were experienced in the world inhabited by them, comprehensible and somehow controllable. Our own existence and the existence of the world that surrounds us, the sun that rises and sets every day, the cycle of the seasons, the moon phases, which cycle mysteriously coincides with women's menstrual period, the influence over tides and on the growth of plants, all this and much more needed an explanation, a search for a cause that allowed to get through the anguish of not having any control over them. The fear in front of what appears incomprehensible and senseless is the motor that drove to the mythical, religious, philosophical, scientific and artistic thought. To believe with an act of faith that a god created us or that we descend from a mythical ancestor, or to discover the laws of evolution through scientific observation, provides in any case an effective answer to many of our uncertainties, just as the shaman's ritual does when he operates on the sick person or the mystical experience that liberates from the burden of materiality and mortality.

To sum up, we can affirm that anthropology is interested in how men, organized in social groups, tried in the past just as nowadays, to have control over their destiny; while psychology focused its interest on the ways of being in the world of the individuals. Differently from ethology, biology and genetics that have as subject matter the observation of living beings in general, anthropology and psychology study human beings; an animal provided with language, even if in some cases not yet able to write, but with a reasoning mind able to communicate to his fellows and to ponder over himself or his own being in the world.

Even though some scientists succeeded in proving the existence of a certain modality of communication based on sounds of different frequencies among some marine mammals as dolphins and whales, only human beings obtained the ability to speak, to share and to hand down stories, concepts and meanings from one generation to another. So, the acquisition of the spoken language establishes an evolutionary leap of immense scope because it put us in a position to memorize and communicate a quantity of information vastly greater than that one possible with only body language or with the limited information transmitted by the sounds signals more or less modulated.

"In the beginning was the Word" so the Bible reads. In Latin "word" is *Verbum* which actually has less meaning of the original Greek term *Logos,* that includes the meanings of word, thought and reason. So it's the "word" that makes us human and like God or, to be more precise, makes it possible to describe God as similar to us. It is not by chance that this God, in order to punish men for their presumption of building a tower high enough to reach heaven, mixes up the languages, bringing them back to an almost "primitive" state, depriving them of the capability of communicating with each other.

"Domine non sum dignus...", "Lord, I am not worthy that Thou should enter under my roof, say but the word, and my soul shall be healed." The ancient Latin missal highlighted, in an extremely efficient way, the

power of the word, especially if it is pronounced by a god. To repeat incessantly a word or a sequence of words in a ritual phrase, as it happens for mantras or in the rosary, allows us to build a bridge between the divinity and us and to appease the anguish of feeling lonely in the universe. But if it's true that we can heal with words, as proven by the prayer and psychotherapy, we know that in turn they can also make us sick. We know the symbolic efficacy of a good wish or a blessing, but a curse or an "evil eye" could be just as efficient when pronounced by someone believed to have a certain power of a diabolic or divine investiture. In Ancient Rome these "magic" words, considered to be able to influence the reality of things and to change it, were engraved on lead or clay boards, called *tabellae defixionis*, and then thrown into the Tiber or into the recipient's well to damn him to bad luck. Among the tortures to which the Inquisition convicted the heretics who used a language to propagate their creed, it was contemplated, together with other terrible mutilations, to cut of the tongue. The Evil News countervails the Good News. In the melodramatic opera "*Cavalleria Rusticana*", Santuzza curses Turiddu dooming him to a terrible destiny with the fatal words: "*A bad Easter to you!*".

As the anthropologists proved in their observations on multiple cultures, every thing believed to be true by the community is in any case real for the effects that it produces, whether they are the consequences of an evil eye, the healing produced by a shamanic ritual or a miracle bestowed by San Gennaro of Naples. As we will see later, the power of suggestion is nowadays abundantly employed by publicity and the placebo effect, for which a sugar pill prescribed as a powerful drug by a doctor succeeds in healing us, allows the pharmaceutical industry to commercialize products lacking real efficacy, achieving huge earnings.

Differently from all the other animal species, the human being has learned, with the development of the larynx and of specialize cerebral areas, to use words and with them, to assign a name to things and all phenomenons of reality. Furthermore, with the use of language it is possible to gather and divulge information, often using images such as those dating back to the Neolithic, drawn in caverns or those frescoed on the walls of Christian Churches to illustrate the evangelical stories to the illiterate masses. So, all that was learned was handed down from one generation to another in the beginning orally and later through writing; an *invention* that allowed us to make a great evolutionary leap to our current level of civilization.

The acquisition of language permitted us to "tell" others, orally or in writing, everything that had been culturally acquired, to share it and hand it down to the following generations, but also *to lie,* a circumstance impossible to be observed in the animal world. Using the metaphor of the expulsion from Eden of our progenitors for having eaten the forbidden fruit of the tree of knowledge, disobeying the divine will, the spoken language brought along a conviction: to deceive and to be deceived; to experience an emotion, to feel it on your skin and in the bowels, just as the blush on your cheeks caused by embarrassment but to deny it or to define it differently with words.

Mystification is the term that the English psychiatrist Ronald Laing used in the 1960s to define this communicative modality pathogenic and potentially devastating when used systematically by a parent towards his own child: to verbally define oneself and the other in an incongruous manner against what we feel and perceive, inducing confusion or, worse, guilt in our counterpart.

Laing tells of a mother who visited her adolescent son, hospitalized in a clinic for mental disturbances. As soon as the boy saw her at the bottom of the hallway, he ran happily towards her, stopping wheezing in front of her and trying to hug her. But his mother instinctively drew back, stiffening for fear; her son was stuck, confused as she immediately reproached him: "Why are you afraid of hugging me?". The boy had a new psychotic crisis and was locked up in confinement. In this regard, it's interesting to report the results of a study on some neurological patients afflicted with aphasia, executed and mentioned by Oliver Sacks in his book "The Mind's Eye". Aphasia is a serious disturbance, linked to specific cerebral lesions, for which an individual loses partially or totally the capability of producing and understanding the language. Words, syntax, grammar have no more meaning to him. These people compensate for their loss of speech by increasing their ability to "reading" the non-verbal signals as facial expressions, body posture and other small revealing gestures, gathering, in this way, the genuine emotional states of the counterpart independently of what he is actually declaring. Because of this ability, they are sometimes employed by the FBI to unmask liars.

To deceive others, especially the ones whom we are sentimentally attached to, makes us feel more powerful and complacent in our narcissism. But to discover of being deceived by someone who should have loved and protected us, represents a serious trauma and causes great suffering. This explains why many individuals, surviving serious interpersonal traumas and socially isolated people as the homeless and the so called punk beast, succeed in establishing strong emotional bonds with an animal that they keep always close to them and that, not able to lie, will never betray them.

To end this preface, following a reflection on the concepts of "normality" and "context".

We are brought to define "normal" the behaviors and the beliefs shared by the majority of the individuals in our social context. Furthermore, we tend to attribute a positive value, to these beliefs and behaviors as if they were absolute laws and consequently natural, whereas we label the ones executed by individuals who are eccentric or belonging to other communities and cultures as oddities or, even worse, barbarity. Actually, the concept of normality is derived from the model of statistics distribution that characterized the majority of the expressions of the physical, biological and social phenomenons, called Gauss' normal curve. This bell-shaped curve (fig.1) displays the distribution of the majority of the values of the examined phenomenon (about 70 percent) around a median central value while the remainders arrange themselves, decreasing rapidly, on the right and on the left side of this central slot.

For example, if we submit one hundred, or one thousand, individuals at random to a blood test to evaluate the cholesterol level, we will find that very few of them will have a very low or very high level, the others will place themselves on intermediate levels while the majority will fall within the slot of central values considered normal indeed. But the central value so established will not represent the "normal" level of cholesterol absolutely, but only the normal one for the population of the examined individuals. If we expand this or other biological values as the blood pressure, or the presence of a certain enzyme to the different populations of the earth, we could discover that what is the normal for one community, isn't for another. So, the concept of normality is connected, in general, with the values expressed by the majority and with the consequent social consensus.

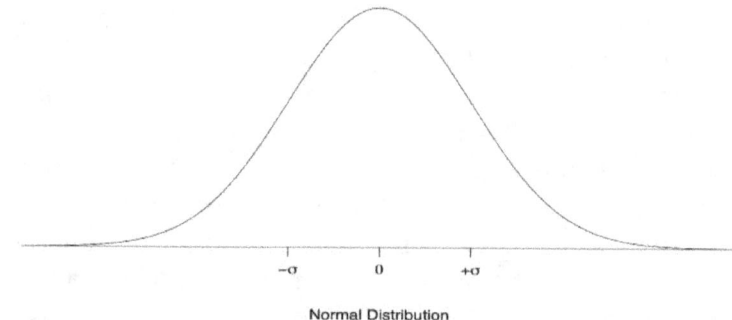

Normal Distribution

Fig.1

We can define context all that surrounds us, from the physical environment to the social and cultural one, and that gives a meaning to our thoughts and behaviors. So, we can speak about social and domestic context, working and professional context, but also in a romantic context, for instance an evening in the moonlight that, as we know, or at least should remember, leads to a seductive behaviors with a final sexual approach. Context and normality are two concepts strictly connected: the context establishes a series of emotions, thoughts and actions that the majority, in that circumstance, considers normal. Not ending the aforementioned romantic soiree at least with a kiss, will risk to appear like a strange behavior, abnormal indeed, inevitably inducing various interpretations in relation to it. So, while we consider sane and normal to wash our private parts, closed in our bathroom, we look with suspicion or derision, if not with fear, a person busy in doing the same thing in the open at a watering hole or at a public fountain, as once some populations so-called primitive used to do or as sometimes now happens to some populations during an emergency circumstance.

Therefore, to pray collectively before a colored chalk statue of a veiled woman, imploring aid to resolve a problem, or to claim a strictly personal guardian angel, designated to protect us for our lifetime, may appear normal or, better yet, laudable. We consider insane a man who claims to see a big white rabbit close to him and moreover who claims to speak affably to him, as it happened to James Stewart in the 1950 film "Harvey". In regards to this, Freud observed very perceptively that religion is a collective psychosis, while psychosis is an individual religion.

What we've just said, helps us to understand how it isn't useful to determine a strict divide between normality and deviance, good and evil, sane and insane but to consider, instead, the social, cultural and psychological manifestations of the human being in the course of its existence as a *continuum* of different strategies of adaptation in a certain context, all worthy of attention and comprehension.

Darwin

In 1543, year of his death, the book "*De Revolutionibus orbium coelestium*" by Nicolaus Copernicus was published. This scientist succeeded in proving, with mathematical procedures, what some Greek philosophers had already foreseen; namely, that it isn't the Earth to be at the centre of the universe but the sun, around which all the planets revolve. This revolutionary theory smoldered for almost a century, until another great thinker, Galileo Galilei, divulged it with his scientific work "*Dialogo sopra i due Massimi Sistemi del Mondo*" drawing the not benevolent attention of the Catholic Church that saw in this the geocentric theory, affirmed by the Bible, wiped out. The cosmic model of Ptolemy and Aristotle that had endured uncontested for centuries put the Earth at the centre of the universe; around it there were some solid sphere among which the planets were set; and the most external sphere contained the stars. Beyond it there was only God that, as a static motor, made everything move. In 1600 Giordano Bruno's assertion of freedom of thought, capable of bringing the articles of faith into question through the scientific investigation, were cause for cutting of his tongue and to burn at stake for heresy, while Galileo Galilei had to renounce his work before the Inquisition Tribunal in 1633 to escape the same fate. By now the seeds had been placed and nowadays, after a few centuries, no one is frightened to think that we and the Earth that we live in, aren't at the centre of the universe.

Two centuries later, an analogous "copernican" revolution, that called into question much more than the old geocentric theory was the publication in 1859 of "On the Origin of Species" by Charles Darwin. In this work, Darwin formulated the results of his meticulous and acute naturalistic investigations carried out in numerous places visited during his long journey around the world on board of the brigantine Beagle. The examination of fossils and of the different characteristics of animals encountered during his explorations, especially those stationed on the Galapagos islands, convinced him that every living species has to adapt itself as well as possible in order not to die in the environment in which it lives and that this adaptation occurs through a natural selection, in the course of the evolution, of the most favorable mutations among those that accidentally occur over generations. Because of their distant position from the South American continent, Galapagos islands have been protected for million years from the external influences of other ecosystems. For that reason the animals that lived there could develop specific morphological characteristics for each single habitat and give rise to a great diversity of species. That's why they were named by the researchers "the living laboratory, showcase of the evolution".

So, the darwinian law of evolution represents the premiss to understanding the origin of all living species, from the first primordial cell capable of reproducing to the most complicated organisms placed at the apex of this ascent, namely ourselves: Homo Sapiens. Charles Darwin was the naturalist scientist that in the nineteenth century, with his works "On the Origin of Species" and "The Descent of Man", lead to a radical revolution in the study of all life sciences, determined by Copernicus and Gallileo Galilei in physics and astronomy.

To accept the scientific evidence of darwinism and consequently to refuse Creationism, a pseudoscientific doctrine, adopted only to remain coherent with the book of the Genesis, which attributes the creation of the universe and of the different life forms on Earth, to God, doesn't necessarily mean to exclude a divine intervention, but to identify God with Nature itself, as suggested by many philosophers, as Lucretius and Spinoza, and many current scientists.

Let's try to understand, by degrees, how the mechanism of evolution by natural selection works. Almost everybody knows the concept of probability, or law of large numbers, for having played poker or bingo. We know that it is only by chance what numbers are extracted just as it is again by chance the choice of bingo cards selected by players before starting the game. Otherwise, playing the Lottery every week, we can choose to use the strategy of betting the same numbers again and again, even for many years, or betting each time on a different string of numbers, chosen at random. We probably have also heard or read somewhere, the notion that placing a chimpanzee before a typewriter for an immeasurable time, almost an infinite time, and by him hitting the keys at

17

random, finally he could casually compose, the Divine Comedy.

Certainly, such law as the fortuitous generation of events reported into the just mentioned examples - extraction of numbers or distribution of cards and, least of all, apes that hit a keyboard - could never have been sufficient alone to generate the magnificent complexity of the living world. Therefore, it becomes necessary to take into account a second element, capable of introducing in the results of a casual production of biological mutations a selective criterion that permits to save and preserve every "useful" combination, discarding all the others. If we come back to Bingo, we notice that the extracted numbers aren't recalled and can't be played again, so at each extraction the successive number has a greater probability than earlier one to be extracted. Furthermore, two numbers in the same row vertically, horizontally or diagonally on the card can be useful to me in the successive extractions to obtain a third in a row, then a forth in a row and so on until I a reach Bingo. In the same way, if playing poker I already have a three of a kind in my hands, while my opponent has just a pair, I keep it, calling only two more cards. The probability, although not the certainty, of winning the hand is certainly mine. Something similar happens to the natural selection in which every little casual mutation that is produced from one generation to another is submitted to a strict examination of the context: if it is useful or, in any case, not damaging, in other words if it produces a best adaptation in terms of survival at least until the reproductive age, it is pre-

served and passed down to the following generations; otherwise, it is eliminated forever with the
premature death of the organism in which it has been
produced. So, the best capabilities of adaptation can
be passed down to the successive generations that
will be selected in respect of the same mechanism.

An objection often promoted by some advocates of
the veracity of the Bible in regards to the divine creation of our progenitors Adam and Eve, affirms that a
so complex organ as, for example, the human eye
can't originate from casual mutations but implies the
intervention of an higher intelligence. However, they
forget to consider a fundamental dimension: the time
factor.

The path from the simplicity of the first unicellular
organism able to reproduce until it arrived to the
complexity of the animal Man fulfilled on the Earth in
more than three billion years. The evolution and the
selection of the natural environment proceeded very
slowly by trials and errors, rewarding and preserving
each time, in the fight for life, those modifications favorable to it, just as a mountain climber does, by
placing one small step after another, in order to reach
the mountain peak, careless of the amount of time it
will take.

*Richard Dawkins illustrated magnificently this
mechanism in his book "Climbing Mount Improbable".
(New York: W.W. Norton & Company. 1996). For a
complete and plain dissertation about the evolution
theme, read also the volume "River out of Eden: A*

Darwinian View of Life"   By Richard Dawkins, New York: Basic Books. 1995.

Genetics and context

Every day we hear about DNA. We learn from news chronicles that each one of us is made up of a unique and specific type, called genome, to the extent that its detection and analysis have replaced, in the procedures of identification, the ones based on the comparison of fingerprints. Every living being, both belonging to the vegetal and animal world, contains DNA in the form of long spirals entangled in themselves called chromosomes that are contained in turn in all the cells of the organism, whether they are only one or thousand of billions as those of our body.

DNA, whose structural model was discovered in the 1950s by Watson, Crick and Wilkins, who obtained together the Nobel prize for their research, was called the alphabet of life, just as the atoms of which all the matter of the universe is composed of are called the alphabet of chemistry. In fact, aside from going deeper into biochemical descriptions irrelevant for our purpose, a parallelism exists between the language and DNA.

Language is composed of a little more than twenty letters of the alphabet that combined variously with each another generate words, concepts, sentences and books, and DNA composed of four basis organic molecules named Adenine, Cytosine, Thymine and Guanine which combined variously with one another create complementary couples and then aggregate in very long strands named genes, joined and inter-

21

twined like a double helix of chromosomes that give rise to the whole genome, that will univocally characterize the living organism that host it.

Similarly, the twelve different notes that constitute the musical scale can combine variously with one another, producing musical arrangements, single musical phrases, melodic themes and entire symphonies.

So, the DNA that constitutes our genetic heritage, in double helix form, is contained in forty-six chromosomes that we have in all body cells, except the reproductive ones, the gametes, which contain only twenty-three chromosomes, that is half. In the fertilized egg they will become again forty-six, half brought by the male sperm and the other half by the female egg. DNA contains the instructions to codify proteins so that from the starting embryo, a fetus develops during gestation and will gradually develop, to a completed entity: in our case a human being. So each of us is "fabricated", in respect to the information included in the genes inherited by half from each of our parents, by a quarter from our four grandparents, by an eight from our great-grandparents and so on. The reality is a little more complicated; in the sense that DNA doesn't cut itself in this way and it may be subject to mutations from one generation to another but we can consider valid this simplification.

Then, the characteristics of the whole living worlds, plants, animals, bacteria and viruses, are inscribed in the genes. Many our genes in the DNA are in common with those of a chimpanzee (almost ninety-nine percent), of a rodent or of a puffer fish, to prove that the whole biosphere originates from a single original molecule that became capable of reproducing and evolving.

So, reproduction is the mechanism that allows the transmission of our own genes to the successive generations and it can be asexual or sexual. In the asexual reproduction, typical, for example, of bacteria, an organism produces identical copies of itself; de facto, it implements cloning and the genetic variability in the course of the generations is exclusively determined by autonomous and fortuitous mutations of the genome. In the sexual reproduction, characterized by the mating of two organisms, the creation of a new organism will occur with its own genome constituted by the fusion of the genes of different entities. In this case, the variability is guaranteed by the recombination of genes originated by mating and this recombination might be, as we can foresee, much more creative.

Among the organisms of the same species that reproduce by mating, according to Darwin, an additional kind of selection takes place, the sexual one, finalized not so much as to guarantee the individual survival but the survival of its own genes, to compete and obtain a better reproductive success.

Innumerable films and documentaries show us the more or less ferocious fights between males of many animals, that takes place during the females' period of estrus to obtain the higher rank (alpha male) to assure favors and sometimes the exclusivity of all the females belonging to the group. This selection can be made through fights between individuals of the same gender with the victory of the stronger, but also, in

23

other cases, through the development, usually in the male, of somatic characters or of specific abilities particularly attractive and seductive in the eyes and nostrils of the females, normally very demanding, as in the case of many birds. In other words, as the peacock teaches us, not always the strongest wins but sometimes the most beautiful one. The final result, in both cases, will be that the losers will have little or no opportunity to mate and to pass his own genes down, left excluded in this way from the competition of the progression of life.

Since a few years, with much presumption and little knowledge, we have started to manipulate the sequences in DNA using an extremely sophisticated technology, creating hybrids non-existent in nature called GMO, that is genetically modified organisms, and introducing criteria of "selection" that have nothing to do with Nature. In particular, the genetic alteration of viruses and bacteria to create new and lethal species to use in possible future conflicts, increases the probabilities of our premature extinction, just as the construction of new nuclear power plants.

Let's try now to understand how "context" puts into effects its function of selection on the variability of the possible genetic expressions of each organism.

To describe what context is for us human beings is not simple. Briefly, it's the environment in which we live in; however, this concept of "environment" can't be limited for us to the mere physical space, to the habitat as the ethologists call it. But rather it must include every thing that, *"in any way"*, can influence and determine my behaviors and the perception of

24

myself in the world. So, we could affirm that context is constituted by the external real world in which we live, defined as physical, social and cultural environment, and by the mental representations of this world that each of us fabricates on the base of the behavioral and cognitive strategies necessarily acquired and adopted to develop our survival probabilities to the utmost. Therefore, the physical environment and the culture of the social group in which we are born establish the context that will give a peculiar mark to all our lives.

Fairy tales give us a starting point to examine these strategies.

A very poor woodcutter and his wife, no longer able to feed their two children, Hansel and Gretel, decide to abandon them in the woods, leaving them to their fate. Locked up by an evil witch that wants to fatten them so as to devour them with more gusto, they will finally succeed in freeing themselves, in killing the hag and coming back to their parents and bringing them the treasure stolen from the old woman. Undoubtedly, the gesture of abandoning our children appears incomprehensible and pitiless today; but until the nineteenth century - and probably even later - the extreme poverty in which the majority of peasants and the working class lived in, lead often families to the abandonment of unwanted infants or elders that were no longer self-sufficient to their fate, as they continued to cultivate the hope to live a better life for themselves. The lack of or the ignorance to use any efficient contraceptive system, and the Church's prohibition in using them, led families to conceive and give birth to many children but the majority of them died precociously from disease or malnutrition. The ones who survived, were compelled to work in factories or in the fields at a very early age, which is nowadays comparable to when they start school. The alternative was for them to voluntary leave the family or their forced abandonment by family, as it has been skillfully described by many nineteenth-century writers in their novels.

Unfortunately, nowadays, in many Asian and African nations millions of children are left to themselves because of wars and poverty and are exploited by sadistic tyrants in many ways: employing them in inhuman jobs or selling them for ignoble purposes.

Hansel and Gretel's fairy tale and other similar ones like, "Little Thumb" by Perrault or "The Little Match Girl" by Andersen, dramatically suggest how the life and destiny of a newborn was at that time, the manner in which they came into the world was also connected with the context they lived in, the same is true today. If it could be possible to choose our parents before being reincarnated, as some oriental school of thought affirm, we could maybe intervene in our future. Actually, the genetic patrimony that we inherit and the environment in which we come into the world defines a set of possibilities more or less ample, but closed, within which it is possible to make some choices for personal development.

These fairy tales regarding abandoned children, that at least in many cases end happily, give us the starting point to explore how the genetic heritage of each of us, whatever it is, can fully express itself or

26

not, depending on the environment (house or woods, for example) in which we will grow up. Who knows if Mozart, endowed with a great genius (and good genes), could express all his potential if he was born in the modest cabin of an Austrian woodcutter instead of the comfortable Salzburg house of a prosperous family of musicians?

These examples, that clearly illustrate how the selection works to favor the apt, take into account a nature already subjected to the culture and which in a more explosive way from the origin of the first civilization to nowadays, has gained the upper hand with its technology and its knowledge.

So, nature has made, in the course of time, its selection on the evolutionary process of living beings, plants and animals, allowing the best adapted organisms to live longer and to reproduce. This long path, from primordial cells to the origin of all other living forms, many of which extinct, is called phylogeny and it has been taking place since three and a half billion years. It constitutes the tree of life with its branching. All the anthropomorphic apes and the first hominids, up until the homo sapiens that currently inhabit the planet with more than six billion individuals, originate from one of the last branches. This global "hominisation" of the Earth, occurred in a dozen centuries, a very short geological time, has lead scientists to denominate our era Anthropocene.

Similarly to phylogeny, but in an infinitely shorter time, another kind of evolution occurs every day for all human beings. It is called ontogeny or life cycle, that is the individual development of every living being, from conception to death. This is what we're going to describe and analyze in the following chapters.

The life cycle

The biological cycle of human life is ultimately the same for each person, independently from the environmental and cultural condition in which it occurs. Only concepts, beliefs and customs change in the different cultures that characterize the various populations. But the cycle doesn't begin exactly with birth and doesn't end definitively with death of the individual because he is already important for the community as an embryo in the maternal womb and even more, at least for a certain time period, as a deceased person.

So, let's consider the birth event. The human female gestation lasts on average nine months during which time the embryo, becomes a fetus and after a completely formed baby, protected in the amniotic fluid from collisions and noises of the external world, nourished through the umbilical cord by his mother's blood and cradled by the rhythmic beat of her heart, should be completely safe. However, this complete bond entails some risks: in fact, through the blood the unborn baby receives not only oxygen and nutritious substances but also a part of the toxic substances possibly assumed by his mother, as alcohol, nicotine and drugs; just as he can inherit some diseases (TB, AIDS and so on). Furthermore, the child, even if protected in the maternal womb, can distinctly perceive his mother's moods: if she is calm, distressed or afraid; and from the seventh month on, he can perceive sounds and it seems even scents that come from the external environment. All this means that the socio-cultural context, the physical, sentimental and emotional environment in which the mother lives in during gestation, affects the unborn child considerably. The prenatal psychology is concerned with the development of the intrauterine bond between mother and child and studies its characteristics and implications. In the past parents of engaged couples were very cautious of the family to which their son or daughter were going to become related to. Today this may seem old fashioned but their approval or impediment to the marriage, wasn't something senseless after all if we were to consider the fact that we now know how context and genes are connected, so that a girl coming from a serene family is more likely to have a good bond during her future maternity.

If we were to participate to the delivery of a baby, we can see that often giving birth is a very dramatic event, actually according to the psychoanalyst Otto Rank, it is traumatic; the positive emotions caused by the miracle of the coming into the world of a new life mingles with those pertaining to the "drama" of which we are spectators; a drama played by two co-stars: mother and newborn.

*Otto Rank was one of the most assiduous assistants and disciples of Freud. In 1924 he explained his revolutionary theory for which the detachment between mother and child appears as a primary trauma that will have repercussions during the adult age with every separation event.

Exactly for this reason, in all the so-called primitive cultures, just as in our rural tradition, the delivery event is considered very critical and is managed only by the women of the village; it was normally considered a taboo for men, who were kept away.

To manage more efficiently this critical event, in some populations of different continents, a funny ritual was acted out, denominated "couvade" by the anthropologists, in which the husband took his wife's place soon after delivery, receiving her treatments, feeling often her indispositions for "empathy". According to the observations of ethnologists, by Korava population in India, *"as soon as the woman perceives labour pains, she informs her husband who promptly wears her clothes and marks his forehead with the characteristic sign of women. Then, he withdraws in a dark room where only a dim lamp shines, and lies down in bed, covering himself with a long garment. The new-born baby is washed and laid in bed next to his father. So, tonics, sedatives and other aliments are given not to the mother but to the father. The father is not allowed to leave the bed and all confronts are brought to him"*.

Evidently, even today, the need to participate to such an extraordinary event as the birth of a child, pushes many fathers to attend the delivery of the baby, with the risk of them being attended to and the need to be reanimated because of the great emotion sustained.

This physical and bodily detachment, between the mother and her child, until now tightly joined, better yet fused together, is accompanied by a lot of strain

31

and pain for both. Furthermore, in respect to the other mammals, human beings have a very large head in proportion to the body, because of the volume of the brain that has continued to develop in the course of evolution. However, the female human pelvis hasn't widened in proportion, making today rather difficult the passage of the baby's head through the cervix and vagina. The head is compressed, as well as the body and, once expelled, the baby experiences an abrupt passage coming from a closed, dark, damp, warm and protected environment, into the light of the day or, worse, of a dazzling lamp in a hospital delivery room. At the same time, no longer receiving any oxygen from his mother through the umbilical cord, he has to inhale air into his lungs, expanding them. In the past it was a common procedure "to help" the newborn in taking this first breath, by lifting his feet and giving him a resounding spanking. This controversial habit has been nowadays abandoned almost everywhere and after cutting, with no excessive hurry the umbilical cord, the baby is laid down on his mother's belly, allowing him to continue to perceive the beat of her heart and to emit autonomously his first cry.

In the course of time, every organism has developed and stored into the DNA, the necessary skills to adapt as best as possible to the context with which it comes into the world and thus increase the probabilities of survival. For this reason, for example, when the eggs of see turtles hatch, the little sea turtles "expect" to be on a fine sandy beach a short distance from the water, and their survival instincts will activate through the "expression" of the genes to guide them on the right direction towards the sea and thus to reach salvation. Similarly, a new-born lamb expects to find next to him a mother with milk-filled udders and a whole herd that protects him; while, as we will try to describe better later, the human baby needs to be accepted by a specific protective figure, usually the mother, to remain in very close physical contact in order to receive not only nutrition but mainly warmth, comfort, and with whom to interact.

The manner with which the newborn draws attention to himself, is mainly by crying followed by appeasement, this tends to activate a genetically programmed response in the mother who is drawn to take care of him. After all, as we have certainly experimented several times, this emotional response manifests itself, in a more or less visible form, in all adults. The presence of a child just as the tenderness that is aroused by the visual, olfactory and auditive signals that come from him, is innate and present in all primates and not only in human beings.

These brief considerations permit us to formulate, or rather to highlight, a structural analogy between a computer and a living being in its entirety. A computer assembled with the most sophisticated hardware is practically useless, even if we turn it on, without the information of a program, software, that inserted from the outside can internally build and define a work environment capable of activating it. Once activated, the computer is ready to continue receiving other information and another software, enriching in this way its memory and acquiring in the course of

33

time always new skills. Similarly, an organism biologi-
cally sophisticated and *"potentially"* capable of great
performances both physical and intellectual as the
human being, is practically "turned off" without a context, an environment both physical and sentimental,
cognitive and relational, that can activate it. This
concept is largely defined by the culture that characterizes the human group, as well as by the physical
environment in which this culture developed.

In 1949 release date of " Les Structures
élémentaires de la parentéle", the anthropologist
Claude Levi-Strauss had already realized this mechanism, studying the development of the mental
schemes during the process of growth of the individual in the society. In fact he writes: "...*the thought of
the adult is built around a certain number of structures... which constitute only a part of those that initially are given, in a summary and undifferentiated
manner, to the thought of the child. In other words,
the mental schemes of the adult diverge depending
on the culture and the age to which each of us belongs; however, they are all elaborated from an initial
universal basis, infinitely richer than the one that every particular society has: coming into the world, every
child brings along, in an embryonic form, the total
sum of the possibilities from which every culture and
every period in history choose a limited part in order
to preserve and develop them. Coming into the
world, every child brings along, in the form of
sketched mental structures, the entirety of the tools
that humankind has from ages to define his relations
with the World and his relations with the Others"*.

C. Levi-Strauss was the founding father of the structural anthropology and his most important work is " Les Structures élémentaires de la parentéle" with it the author shows how the kinship relations and the marriage relationship are fundamental, rather "institutional", to the basis of all the social structures developed by human beings. Furthermore, he also analyses the specific attributions of the different roles of the kinship, associated with their denominations. As an example for us, our father's brother and our mother's brother are indifferently called "uncle", but in most cultures these positions are greatly differentiated. In Ancient Rome the paternal uncle was called "Patruus" while the maternal one was called "Avunculus"; because of the patriarchal system of juridical laws of the time, the relationship of the nephew towards the two uncles was quiet different, thus the fathers' bother was much more important and demand grater respect then the uncle on the mother's side, who was regarded more like a friend and a companion.

The society, the family which is its founding nucleus and the quality of the primary relationship mother-son, are similar to the Russian matryoshka dolls or the fractal figures of Mandelbrot that depict the macroscopic into the microscopic, as containers enclosed one inside the other where the bigger one gives form to the others. All together they constitute the filters needed to select the one unique and exclusive development, among all the possibilities potentially existent in the child. It will be the one most capable to adaptation and the most efficient to ensure the survival in that specific context. So, a child deprived of the context would be like an astronaut dispersed in the cosmic space or, to evoke the already mentioned analogy, like a computer deprived of the software.

It is said that in the twelfth century, at the court of Frederick II of Swabia, some dignitaries wanted to prove the thesis that children came into the world with the innate ability to speak and understand one language, Latin, considered the only "natural" one, present for innate predisposition in the child, while all the other languages had to be learned at a later time. To prove this absurd thesis, some newborns were locked in a space completely isolated from the outside world, allowing their mothers and nannies to come in just the time necessary to feed them but never letting these women speak or interact with them in any way. The result was, as they say, that within a few months they all died from neglect and from deprivation of any environmental stimulus, proving they were wrong.

Let's come back now to the theme of the abandoned children soon after their birth. Up until the fifties during the last century, when "civilization" had not yet reached all populations, mass media often reported cases usually occurring in very poor regions of India, China and Amazon of findings savage children who were bred by wolves or apes. We know that such events are frequently reported in myths and folk traditions such as those of the twins Romulus and Remus rescued by a wolf or of the baby Moses entrusted to the waters of the Nile river, which probably

36

inspired R. Kipling's book, *"The Jungle Book"*. The statistics tell us that the majority of the newborns, abandoned, then in the woods and nowadays in the streets, die in a short time. However, there have been cases in the past, abundantly documented, in which the females of some animal species have welcomed an "extraneous" puppy among theirs, allowing him to live. The so-called maternal instinct evidently exists and is present in all mammals; in 1996, in the Chicago zoo, a three-year-old child accidentally fell into the gorillas' enclosure. To the amazement of those present, a female gorilla picked him up, cradled him for a while in her arms to calm him and then brought him to the custodian who had just entered the cage. Obviously she wasn't a trained animal to mechanically perform for a reward!

The most famous case of discovery is that of the child-wolf that wandered for a long time in the woods of Aveyron, in France, in the eighteenth century. He was captured by three hunters and brought to the village tied with much difficulty, because he growled and bit. The young boy was about twelve years old but was short for his age. Obviously he didn't speak and acted exactly like an animal.

The case was handled by many medical scientists including Philippe Pinel, a French doctor who revolutionized psychiatry, he considered the mentally ill person not as a social outcast to lock up in chains but as human being to be cured through the construction of a personal relationship and through rehabilitation; for his way of thinking he anticipated psychotherapy by many years.

The boy was brought to Paris and studied for several years, trying to teach him the language and some basic behaviors, but with zero results. With a mechanism similar to imprinting studied by K. Lorenz, Victor, the name given to the boy, had built a mental image of himself, of the significant others and of the world surrounding him on the basis of what he had learned during his first years of life spent together with the wolves and he had totally lost the capability of identifying himself as a member of the human species. A similar case was the discovery in the Indian jungle, in 1920, of two little girls abandoned by their mother and survived thanks to the adoption by a pack of wolves.

Konrad Lorenz, the Austrian scientist, awarded with the Nobel Prize for Physiology and Medicine in 1973, was the founder of the modern ethology. The imprinting phenomenon observed by him, that will greatly influence J. Bowlby in the elaboration of his attachment theory, is a form of strict learning, present in various degrees in all vertebrates, that is activated at birth within a defined and limited time period. Subjects of his studies were the wild ducks of the Danube. When the eggs hatch, the little ducks normally memorize, as a trade-mark, the image of the mother that has brooded them; from that moment on they will identify themselves as members of her species and will follow her. Lorenz, introducing himself into their environment, pretended he was their mother at the moment of their birth. They "identified" themselves in him and followed him from that mo-

ment on; when they were adult, they continued to believe in being members of the human species to the point of trying to mate with humans instead of other ducks.

None of the wild children found extraordinarily in India and in other countries up until a few decades ago, have ever been able to blend into society in any way, even with all the efforts put into place by scientist. Once the time slot that goes from birth to the first three years of life is closed, it appears hardly modifiable in its contents, similarly to the ROM memory (read-only memory) that receives only once the information from the surrounding environment, but after having recorded the essential data for the *survival in that context*, it can no longer be modified. This is more and more true when we descend down the evolutionary ladder; Lorenz's ducks that, at the time when the eggs had hatched, had "identified" the scientist as their mother through the imprinting mechanism, were never able to identify themselves as ducks.

The captivating mystery of the close interaction that exists between the genetic patrimony and the environment is currently object of the study of many researchers and a new scientific field has been singled out called epigenetic; it literally means "over genetics", which studies the causes of changes in the organism not attributable to changes in the genome.

We have seen that in the nineteenth century Darwin proved with the scientific method that the changes traceable in the course of time in the living species are the result of accidental gene mutations, acquired permanently and passed down to the successive generations or soon eliminated depending on the positive or negative value for the survival of the organism in the environmental context. The most quoted example that illustrates this phenomenon is the one related to an English moth, the (Biston Betularia).

This night-flying moth was white until the mid-nineteenth century; which in a short time after the so called industrial revolution in England, turned dark, almost black. The explanation comes from the fact that this moth, a nocturnal insect, that during the day sleeps leaning against the trunks of birch trees can be prey of various species of birds. The birch cortex, before pollution of the coal due to the industrialization, was whitish and the white moths through camouflaging survived much more efficiently than the dark ones, thus they reproduced in greater numbers. From 1850 to the first half of 1900, because of the coal pollution, the birch cortex darkened more and more and so the white butterflies thinned out, giving way to the dark ones, since they now became more adapted to the new context. The gene that determined the dark coloring in the moths proved to be successful in terms of adaptation.

A few years before Darwin developed his theory of evolution, the French naturalist Jean Baptiste de Lamarck hypothesized the acquisition and the transmission of physiological alterations from a functional improvement of the organism in response to the pressures of the environment to the following generations. The example that he brought in support of his theory was the giraffe; originally it didn't have a long neck, but to reach the higher branches of the trees from which it acquired nourishment, it needed to stretch its neck higher and higher, till over time it reached its long form, thus allowing the descendants to acquired permanently the length of the neck as we see it today. Similarly, an improved night sight, developed by an individual in the course of many years of work in an environment deprived of natural light like a mine, would be passed down directly to his children.

Lamarck's thought hypothesized an innate impulsion towards a gradual improvement of adaptation to the environment present in all animals and achieved through the development or the regression of particular organs or body parts.

According to Darwin it was chance that determined variations in the organisms and these changes passed down to the descendants only in respect to their abilities to improve considerably the possibilities of survival and reproduction, establishing firmly themselves as new characteristic of the species only after many generations. According to Lamarck instead, each organism by nature tends to evolve or to regress in order to take the best advantage of the environment in which it lives, then passes down these changes, finalized to a specific aim, to its descendants.

Epigenetic seems today to reconcile these two evolutionist theories only partially opposed. It was found, in fact, that some genes inherited by each organism, even if they are practically unchangeable in their DNA sequence, can be activated or inhibited in their expression, by means of a complicated biochem-

41

ical operation, by stressful factors coming from the environment; furthermore, these inhibited genes can be passed down unaltered to the successive generations.

To make an immediately comprehensible example: if during a long famine (environmental pressure) my grandparents were able to survive developing the ability to use better and more efficaciously the scarce food resources available through the modification of their metabolism (attained through the activation or the inhibition of specific genes present in our own genome), I may have inherited the above ability. This could allow me, for example, to be better protected from the risk of cardiovascular diseases or diabetes.

Furthermore, a research of the University of Zurich proved that mice, deprived of the maternal support soon after their birth, not only developed serious depressive symptoms with consequent alterations of the cerebral activity but, once adult, they will also pass them down, by genetic means, to their offspring. This mechanism of interaction between genetics and environment is providing glimmers for the understanding and the treatment of the so called PTSD (Post Traumatic Stress Disorders), that is the effects of the serious traumas suffered by the individuals and the possible transmission of these effects to their descendants.

This seems to scientifically confirm what the systemic and relational psychotherapists, in their work with problematic families, had guessed and verified since the 50s during the past century, namely that a serious trauma occurred, many years before to a member of a family could continue to produce its dramatic effects on his unaware descendants even after three or four generations. Nowadays, various psychotherapeutic approaches resort to the recovery and the narration of the patients family history to intervene more effectively with the healing process.

The attachment theory

We mentioned in the previous pages how an innate predisposition, inscribed in the DNA, can be moulded, inhibited or enhanced by the environment in which it occurs. In primates and mainly in humans, the influence of the context on the modalities of expression of the innate behavioral schemes is maximum, whereas in other animals these schemes become more and more strict and unchangeable as we descend down the evolutionary ladder. Let's think of the spider's web: it appears perfect, functional, almost a proof of its intelligence. But the spider's behavior is rigidly programmed to the point that in every situation in which the web is destroyed, it is always rebuilt in the same manner without the possibility of any changes. In the case of a farm animal, if we were to put a metal net barrier between a hen and the maize: the hen will continue to uselessly bump into the net in the attempt to reach the corn. A dog or a cat instead, placed in the same situation before a tasty morsel of food, after one or two failed attempts will learn to go around the barrier in order to reach it and, in a similar circumstance will put into use the new behavior learned, without making any more false attempts. Therefore, the acquired knowledge that comes from the context experience, can modify the innate patterns of action. This becomes more evident as we move up on the evolutionary ladder of living beings.

The attachment theory developed in the 1950s through the observations of J. Bowlby on the phases of mourning elaborated by human beings and the ethological studies on small primates (Rhesus monkeys) conducted by H. Harlow. In those years Mary Ainsworth led a study in Uganda on the premature interactions observed in the mother-child relationship and Bowlby started a retrospective study on forty-four adolescent and antisocial thieves in London, discovering that most of them came from poor and broken families in which they had grown up practically abandoned to themselves.

Harlow, along with his wife, conducted a test where by he separated eight little Rhesus monkeys from their mother soon after their birth and placed them in a cage inside which he had placed two metal simulacra the size of an adult ape. One of them held a baby's bottle full of lukewarm milk, while the other one without the baby's bottle, was clothed in a soft fur that imitated the maternal body of the ape. The little Rhesus, deprived of maternal care, preferred to cling tenaciously to the plush "mother" to find comfort, whereas they went to the metal "mother" only for the short time necessary to be fed. The Harlows at the end of their experiment realized that the primary need of the puppies was not the food but the availability of a caring adult to cling to and with which to interact. Furthermore, they observed that when the little monkeys were scared, they ran to the plush mother, looking desperately for protection and comfort but yet remained frightened and anguished because the fake mother couldn't interact with them or give them reassurance as a real ape mother would do through her eye contact and her voice. Once adult and reintegrated in the original group, all the apes, who had undergone the experiment, manifested aggressive and antisocial behaviors and proved to be bad mothers with their own puppies. The Harlows' experiment anticipated without a doubt what Bowlby proved to be valid for humans too: that a child from   birth manifests the primary need to have a mother that is able to embraces him and take care of him actively and not only a nipple to suckle on.

Bowlby was also impressed by a research carried out in the suburbs of London, that showed the close correlation between the inclination of adolescents to break laws and the social and domestic inadequate and degraded context, characterized by the deprivation of maternal cares. A few years before, Anna Freud, Sigmund's daughter, while assisting in a British hospitals some orphans of war, was impressed by the psychic and physical consequences on children caused by the lack of a stable relationship with the maternal figure; and she used the direct observation and not just the narrations of adult patients about their childhood, to prove the effectiveness of the psychoanalytical theories conducted by her father.

In addition, the observations on the field of the ethologists and anthropologists, since the nineteenth century, highlighted how in all the human groups the mother-child bond appeared always very strong and is based on body contact, from birth to following three years of life and beyond. The photos and drawings depicted by them, showed the child in very close

46

contact with his mother, placed in a bag at her side from where, whenever he wanted, could easily have access to his mother's bosom, or brought in a sort of backpack or wicker basket on her back, even when she was busy working in the fields or in other tasks. (fig.2)

In clockwise direction, women of Fiji islands, China, India, Africa (fig.2)

It was clear that such a close bond made the child feel safe and relaxed; consequently, he rarely had a tantrum or showed himself upset for very long. In the fifties anthropologist C. Levi-Strauss writes about the natives of Amazon: *"The spectacle of a mother with her child is full of joviality and freshness. When they are vexed, the children often beat on their mother and she doesn't react. They are never punished and I have never seen one being beaten or even make the gesture, if not for play. Sometimes a child cries because he is hurt, he had a fight, he was hungry or he doesn't want to be deloused. But the latter case is rare: the delousing seems to enchant the patient as much as it amuses the executor; it is considered as a sign of interest and affection."*

In other words, the well-established orthodox psychoanalytic theory that hypothesized a child pushed by his internal narcissistic "impulses" (oral, anal, phallic) to fantasize incestuous and parricidal scenarios, called Oedipal theory, was definitively falsified by the scientific observations, even transcultural as those made by the anthropologist Margaret Mead in Samoa and New Guinea and by Ainsworth in Uganda, that revealed how a child is orientated since his birth to look for warmth, physical contact and self-confidence in a maternal figure and he is brought to interact with her vivaciously to obtain them. Many decades passed from the disclosure of the first Freudian theories before psychology started to focus the attention on the role of the early lived experiences in the genesis of the so-called neurosis and psychosis and no longer on the fantasies. The attachment is for Bowlby a *primary motivational system,* the activation of which corresponds with a *behavior of attachment* (recalls, cries, clinging). These behaviors are functional to invoke the mother's closeness and are triggered by the threat of separation or other frightening events, experienced in the course of the first explorations of the child, for example, a loud sudden noise or the pain caused by the impact with a solid and hard object. The prompt response of the mother with her care and her protective attitude, not just occasional but stable over time, will allow the child to build confidence in himself and in others. Bowlby has named this, with profound perception, "a safe base".

So, the boost that springs the attachment system is fear; the behavioral response associated with it is the active search of protection in the caring figure (care-giver) usually the mother. But the *care-giver may* not even be the biological mother, as in the case of newborns given in foster care or adoption, or entrusted to the care of a nanny as once was customary in the middle-class families.

For the sake of simplicity, we will continue to identify the figure of the care-giver in the mother.

So, we can restate that the primary needs of the child are protection and security and that these are actively demanded specifically through intense crying, when he feels in danger. In fact, as it occurs for the majority of the mammals puppies, the distance from the mother is perceived as a lack of defense from external dangers, whether it is from a possible predator or death caused by neglect. While for many of animals security is identified with a specific place as the den, for apes and for the majority of primates, including the human beings, safety is achieved only through the close physical contact with the maternal figure.

The sense of security allows us to be serene and calm; whereas any perception of threat triggers the defense system, that leads the child to move away from the danger situation, if he can, and at the same time, triggers the attachment system that brings him to immediately look for maternal protection. This double innate response to danger signals, highly efficient and selected by evolution in the course of time, in some cases can cause an unsolvable internal conflict. As we have seen, the defense system pushes the child to immediately step back from the danger or distressing circumstances, while the attachment system pushes him to search for the maternal figure. The two systems are triggered simultaneously and when danger is external, they act synergistically to provide an efficient and appropriate defensive response. But if the source of danger for the child turns out to be his own mother, in a situation occurring over time, it can cause serious psychic problems during the course of development and in adulthood.

Now, let's go back to the attachment system. The manner in which this primary need will receive a response by the maternal figure, will mould in a short time, the child's behavior and his expectations. While the impulse to look for food, warmth and security pushes some animals to take shelter in their den where they will always be welcomed, unless it is destroyed by a predator, the same impulse will bring a child to look for his mother. The mother in turn may respond in many different manners, in general and in the majority of times, her response will be positive but in some cases she may response negatively, and in other limited cases she may respond by refusing or mistreating him.

To summarize the highlights of the attachment system:

1. *Monotropism, is* intended as a preferential bond with a specific single figure, usually the mother. In the absence of the mother, the child can turn to other adult figures for help, as it occurs in all extended families in which the children are looked after by the other women of the house and thus they can develop multiple attachments.

2. *Safe base.* The prompt maternal response to the child's requests for care, creates in a short time, a feeling of generalized and internalized safety defined "safe base". When the awareness of a safe internal base is not created in the child, the normal behaviors of exploration will be abandoned and constant maneuvers of defense will be employed against the fear of abandonment, as for example anxious clinging to the mother.

3. *Protests*. A child manifest his protest against the threat of separation, through rage followed by sadness.

Therefore, within the first three years of life, a specific type of attachment, built on the basis of the actual interactional experiences with the maternal figure, is established and consolidated in the child. The child "mirrors" himself in his mother's eyes, consequently building a mental representation of himself and of the other one with whom he is in relationship with; in brief, he builds over time and memorizes meanings and beliefs about himself (I'm good, I'm wicked, I'm amiable, I'm capable, I'm not worth a dime, I'm incapable) and about others (they are reliable, they are dangerous, they can help me, they reject me). These beliefs and the consequent relational behaviors have been defined by Bowlby "Internal Working Models" (IWM). As we will see, they are very different according to the type of attachment that the child will develop and they will influence in the course of time every affective bond that he will build or will try to build. To sum up, there is an immutable biological fact: the child grows in the womb, he is given birth and, if all goes well, is breastfed by his mother. Their bond is called *primary* because it begins to form already during pregnancy. He not only is fed and oxygenated by her blood, but from a certain point onwards he will also begin to perceive the beat of her heart, her moods and to listen together with her, music and sounds and even scents from the outside world. From birth to the third year of age, through the actual experiences of interaction with the maternal figure, the child develops a specific method to relate to her when he needs to be reassured, supported and comforted.

Mary Ainsworth developed a particular test, called *Strange Situation,* to observe and define three main types of attachments as: *Secure Attachment, Insecure Avoidant and Insecure Ambivalent.* Given that after eighteen months the attachment is already structured in the child, the test is mainly carried out on subjects of this age. Briefly described, the experi-

52

ment consists in observing the reactions of the child, when he is first placed in a comfortable room together with his mother, later by creating a new circumstance that becomes potentially stressful as the entrance of a stranger and the walking away of his mother followed by her coming back in the room after a few minutes.

Thereafter, the American psychologist Mary Main and other researchers identified a forth type of attachment that was called *disoriented - disorganized* and grouped in the Strange Situation those children that behaved exactly in an unpredictable and incoherent manner.

Types of attachment.

1. *Secure Attachment* or type B. In this type of attachment the child feels secure every time his needs are met with a warm and protective response by his mother. In other words, the mother is always in an emotional and cognitive *harmony* with her child and in *synchrony* with his rhythms. Submitted to the Strange Situation test, these children can also vivaciously protest against separation with outcries, but when their mothers come back they run towards them confident that they will be immediately reassured.

2. *Insecure Avoidant Attachment* or type A. In this case the need of reassurance is devalued, denied or removed; in experiencing a mother sentimentally cold or unhelpful, the child reacts "contenting himself" with what little he succeeds in obtaining, learning to avoid any insistent requests of physical and emotional contact that would cause a further estrangement in his mother. In the "Strange Situation" the child doesn't

cry and seems almost not to notice that his mother has left the room. When she comes back in the room, he shows indifference and tends to avoid contact, turning his head elsewhere or maybe pretending to be interested in a toy, but his physiological parameters, measured soon after the separation, indicate the presence of stress (rapid heartbeat, perspiration). As these children grow they appear independent and very armored against the anguishes of separation but this strategy of adaptation is based on the separation of emotions from consciousness: the anger resulting from the lack or inadequacy of response to the primary needs of affection and protection is initially removed and after denied and cut off from themselves. The emotions not displayed to the attachment figure can be diverted on less important and therefore less dangerous targets or they can arise, especially in adulthood, through the wide range of psychosomatic disorders.

3. *Insecure Ambivalent (or resistant) Attachment,* type C. The mother responds to the child's requests in an incongruous manner, maybe with intrusive behaviors by uselessly exciting him when the child doesn't look for her and plays serenely on his own, and on the contrary reacting with neglect when he looks for her because he is frightened or anxious. The characteristic that distinguishes this type seems to be the unpredictability. The child clings worried to his mother, with excessive submission and regressive requests of contact with ambivalent methods. Both the attachment figure and the child seem to find safety through a relationship based on the troubled control of the other.

4. *Disoriented - Disorganized Attachment* or type D. This is the theoretical model developed later by Mary Main to diagnose children, submitted to the Strange Situation test, that didn't fall into the three previous categories defined by Bowlby and Ainsworth.

In the type D, the attachment behavior, activated, as we know, by fear and anxiety, pushes the frightened child to seek refuge in his mother stepping away from the danger. However, in this case, she herself appears as a source of fear. A mother depressed for a recent mourning that still provokes in her agonizing emotions, can physically take care of her child but she will be emotionally distant light years away from him and his from his need for affection. She will appear frightened and unable to reassure him; while in the case that she will be plainly mistreating and abusing, she will evoke in him an irrepressible fear. In any case the attachment figure is perceived as frightening and/or frightened. This situation increases the child's fear, instead of solving or mitigating it, a sort of perverse circle is established with no way out (danger, estrangement, appeal to the mother, and again danger). The child experiences *a fear without any possibility of solution.*

However, the research highlighted other circumstances potentially at risk of consolidating an attachment of this type, like the extreme negligence and the lack of verbal, facial and ocular interaction between the child and his mother, perhaps because she welcomes him mechanically by continuing to watch her favorite program on television.

This type of attachment is highly at risk of psycho-pathological developments also in adulthood. We will examine in depth later the implications of the type D, which is built on traumas repeated over time in a child that cannot escape them. In this case trauma is defined as all the circumstances in which the individual feels his own survival is threatened and for which he can activate the most extreme defenses he has available.

From eighteen months to three years of life the Internal Working Models (IWM) related to the type of attachment develop in the child are structured and become quite mentally stable.

I believe it emerges with extreme obviousness the role played by the learning process in this first phase of the life of an individual.

During a psychiatric conference that took place a few years ago, a story was told which is a powerful metaphor of how our past can influence our present. A father brought his child to the circus and since there was time before the show started, walked with him among the animal cages. Suddenly they saw a huge elephant tied by one foot to a chain that was stuck in the ground at the other end with a big wooden peg. The child observes it carefully and then said to his father: "But such a big animal could free himself easily with a tug from that chain! Why doesn't he do it?" The father ponders for a moment and then answers: "The fact is that this chain that imprisons him was put around his paw when he was a puppy, and at that time he didn't have the strength to free himself. Now that he can, he continues to believe he doesn't have the strength to free himself and doesn't even try to escape!"

Even though it would be improper to consider the child's mind at birth as a "tabula rasa", his first *real* experiences in the relational context in which he belongs to, not only influences the emotional and cognitive development but it also contributes to the formation of a specific mental "map" of the world and to the construction of a specific image of himself and others. Even if the successive experiences can sometimes modify for the better or for the worse these patterns, it was observed that the IWM, related to a type of attachment developed in childhood, remains unaltered in the majority of cases, also in adult life. This means that, in all the important emotional bonds that we will build in the course of our lives, at the activation of the attachment, the internal working models elaborated during childhood will be applied. For example a child classified as insecure avoidant (type A), once adult will have considerable probabilities of becoming a parent of a child that will develop an analogous type of attachment towards him.

Let's remember in this regard that when the attachment system is activated in the child, the corresponding caregiving system is complimentarily activated in the *care-giver* because it's always involved an interaction between the two individuals. So, let's examine the caregiving styles, or rather, the manners of response to the need of security expressed by the child that a mother can provide.

Mary Main and others have developed a test administered to the parents and specifically to mothers, called AAI, Adult Attachment Interview, which in the course of a structured interview reveals the manners of caregiving of the adults, classifying them into four types analogous and symmetrical to the four types of attachment mentioned above. In the course of the interview the adult is asked to narrate her childhood events in order to evaluate the internal coherence together with other parameters. So, more attention is paid to how the story is narrated than to the specific contents itself, which will be in any case submitted for an appropriate evaluation. For this purpose it may be useful to suppose that a parent can be brought to interact with the child, perceiving him as he really is, or as an imaginary child, based upon his fantasies or his need for reparation and unresolved traumas suffered in his own childhood. Daniel Stern, specialist in infant development, makes a very efficient distinction between the real child and the imaginary one, that is between the perception of his own child as he really is and the internal image that a parent build on the basis of his own childhood story and of the consequent desires and expectations placed upon him. The more the perception of his own child is distant from the real child the more his child will be at risk of a problematic development.

In response to the child's request the parent can relate to him in the manners listed below, corresponding to the types of attachment B, A, C, D

Secure/Autonomous. The mother answers adequately to the expressions of child's discomfort, with sensibility, emotional harmony and sentimental warmth. The needs of the real child are understood and they are provided with an appropriate response.

Dismissing/Avoidant. The mother underestimates or doesn't respond to the caregiving requests of the child and she isn't emotionally involved. She can efficaciously take care of him in terms of material needs but neglect his emotional needs or humiliate him when he manifests them.

Preoccupied/Ambivalent. The mother has a controlling and intrusive behavior not in harmony or in synchrony with the child's requests. She can be overprotective, making him insecure and inhibiting his exploration. She often doesn't see the real child but her own internal child that hasn't completely solved the past traumas.

Unresolved/Disorganized. The mother didn't solve the serious traumas and/or mournings experienced in her own past or she is victim of serious stress for contingent situations (alcoholism, domestic violence, psychiatric disorder); she responds in a disorganized and frightening manner to the child's requests, arousing fear without solution in him. The powerful emotions that she can't control and manage along with the unsolved traumatic memories, keep her in the past and prevent her from being anchored to reality, "here and now". This prevents her from emotionally contacting her child that, paradoxically, can be experienced by her as a persecuting ghost which she wants to free herself from.

In regards to the first three relational manners previously described, the child builds in any case an internal image of himself *unitary and coherent*, so not dissociated or fragmented, independently of its positive or negative value that we can thus briefly summarize:

B/Secure-Autonomous: "I am lovable, I'm good".

A/Dismissing-Avoidant: "I'm not lovable, I'm often wicked". I can't and I mustn't rely on the help of the others.

C/Preocupied-Ambivalent: "Sometimes I am lovable and good, sometimes I'm unlovable and wicked".

In type D/Unresolved-Disorganized the child is subject, as we have already described, to a fear without solution because the mother that should protect and reassure him can be perceived, in rapid sequence, as frightening (she is persecutor and he is victim) or scared (she is victim, he is persecutor or both potential victims of an external danger) or in a confused and dissociated mental condition (she is threatened by an external danger and he is the savior); consequently he won't succeed in developing a unitary and coherent image of himself but he will tend to perceive himself *at the same time* victim, persecutor and savior. This mental condition centered on three relational positions in which the child (and later the adult) is in a manner of speaking, trapped in, has been called "dramatic triangle" by the researcher of the Attachment theory Giovanni Liotti and indeed, it consists of three mental representations of the Self and of the Other irreconcilable and not integrated with one another. Furthermore, each time the attachment system is activated, the individual will tend to experience a serious state of anxiety and anguish that, if not adequately managed and restrained, will lead him to dissociate a part of himself, making him feel alien to himself and to the world that surrounds him. As we can guess, this type of attachment predisposes (but doesn't determine) the child and later the adult, to dissociative disorders of the personality.

At a preliminary reading, it would seem that what has been told until now accuses excessively the maternal role, attributing the cause of any pathology that the individual will develop. But the criticality of the primary bond mother-child, from the gestation to the first three years of life, is by now proven and recognized in every field of the psychological sciences. To this effect Bowlby actively proposed governments to enforce labor laws in order to protect working mothers, so that they would be able to stay longer with their children and breastfeed them up to two years of age without having to go back to work immediately. Moreover, the quality of the secondary bonds that he will build with other significant adults, among which obviously the father and the events that he will have to face in the course of his own life, will produce effects on his psychophysical equilibrium. With regards to the ability of dealing with high level stress, having or not built inside himself the famous safe base described by Bowlby, will allow him to overcome any adverse experience without serious damage, or to show a great vulnerability to these.

The father's role.

In our current "western" culture, the paternal figure has acquired an important role from the very first day of birth of the infant, since he is actively involved, alongside the mother, in changing of the diapers, in feeding the baby with the milk bottle, in playtime activities and in cuddles. Therefore, the child develops towards his father an attachment that we could call secondary and that could also be of a different type from that one developed towards his mother. The importance of the father's presence is not only determined by supplying an additional emotional bond to the child, but by the fact that he represents a valuable emotional support, as well as concrete, for his own companion who has just become a mother. The advent of the industrial civilization has erased the so called extended or enlarged family, constituted by at least three generations of individuals who all lived in the same house, as of those in the past in the small farms and in most rural areas and as it is still customary in current cultures not completely "civilized". In these cases, indeed, the woman who gave birth could always count on the material and emotional support of the other women of the family (mothers, sisters, sisters-in-law), while the men, at least as long as the breastfeeding lasted (and it could last two or three years too), tended to keep out on the fringes of the group formed by the women and their children. Today's family instead, formed by only parents and children, who often reside in places relatively far from the grandparents or other relatives, have to face alone the stress of such a destabilizing change of life as the birth of a child. The woman, who had already seen in the early months of her pregnancy the rapid body changes of her image and had to begin to assimilate and manage these changes, with the birth of her child, has to deal with a totally new reality that calls into question not only her own identity and her personal balances but also that of the couple. The concern, the fear and the anxiety that all this produces, will trigger, as we have seen, her attachment system that in case it is secure type, she will tend to elicit and expect an immediate emotional response that is comforting and that makes her feel cared for in an effective manner. This is exactly the task that is required by her companion, especially when, for various reasons, significant female figures who are protective and caring for the woman who has just given birth, as for example her own mother, aren't present.

The so called postpartum depression, characterized by crying crisis, sudden changes of mood, lack of appetite, sleep disturbances and so on, isn't an aleatory event that can target all women who have just given birth, as it is commonly believed, but it's often determined by the activation of the attachment system that isn't followed by an efficient and appropriate response. In the case of secure attachment this lacking or inadequate response can bring on, as we mentioned, to irritability, protests and crying. In other cases of insecure attachment, dysfunctional behavioral manners and emotions correlated with the internal working models that characterized this typology can arise. The puerperal psychosis, which is rather rare, is characterized by a much more serious symptoms and it is thought to be related, among the different factors, to a type D attachment.

Lastly, the attachment system is an innate response to the circumstances that generate fear and anxiety, first of all as a result of a real threat or the fear of losing an emotional bond; and its activation leads to look for a complementary caring figure with the operational manners that we have learned in our first three years of life, interacting with the surroundings. So, to ask to be cared for is an innate need not only during childhood years as we might erroneously think, but the whole duration of our life, we totally learn "how" to ask and "what" to expect from the relationship. Moreover, the primary need of each of us is the achievement and the preservation of a "state of security", composed not only by the availability of food and shelter from weather adversities but mainly by the awareness of not being left alone. Eduardo Galeano*, Uruguayan writer, describes this primary need with a pleasing poem:

In 1974 her bones turned up in the rocky hills of Ethiopia.

Her discoverers called her Lucy.

Thanks to advanced technology, they were able to calculate her age at about three million, one hundred and seventy-five thousand years, give or take a day or two. And also her height: she was rather short, a little over three feet tall.

The rest was deduced or maybe guessed: her body was quite hairy and she didn't walk on all fours, rather she swung along in a chimpanzee walk, her hands nearly grazing the ground, though she preferred treetops.

She might have been drowned in a river. She might have been fleeing a lion or some other unknown who showed an interest in her.

She was born long before fire or word, but perhaps she spoke a language of gestures and sounds that could have said, or tried to say, for example,

"I'm cold,

I'm hungry,

Don't leave me alone".

*E. Galeano, I figli dei giorni, Sperling & Kupfer, 2012. /E. Galeano, Children of the Days, Nation Books, 2013.

Stay alive

In the scale of priorities, the survival instinct is certainly in first place. To fulfill the needs of nourishment and of protection from the external dangers of any kind allows us to extend as much as possible the time of our existence.   But man, ever since a long time ago, with his abilities of abstraction and reflection, has also begun to wonder about the meaning of his existence.

Leaving aside all the innumerable cultural productions with which since thousands of years we have tried to give a fideistic explanation, as myths, religions, philosophy and even science, the question if the laws that govern the universe are part of certain "Intelligent Design", for man still remains to be considered the mere biological fact. The astrophysicist Margherita Hack said *"The task of science is to do without God"*.

So, the two instincts or primary purposes that characterize every living being are to survive as long as possible and to allow its own genes to survive in the course of time, generating a progeny that can in turn survive as long as possible. What interests us is to understand what are the different manners and the culturally determined strategies that humans have developed, individually or in groups, to face the strict impositions of these natural laws, and what are the innate resources, among the many potentially available, that they have decided to use from time to time. Cultural anthropology and psychology have been involved and are involved in observing, describing and studying these strategies.

Since the birth of ancient civilizations, merchants, warriors and travelers reported in their stories, full of wonder and terror, the strange customs and traditions, and sometimes the horrible features, of the foreign peoples with which they had come in contact. Frequently, these contacts led at a later time to profitable commercial and cultural exchanges, but just as frequently entire populations were exterminated and their civilizations were destroyed just for dominion lust, opportunely connoting them from time to time as barbaric, uncivilized or pagan, as it happened, in the course of a few decades of "conquest", with the American great indigenous civilizations. The Enlightenment and later the nineteenth-century Positivism, together with the development of the colonial politics of Great Britain, Spain, Portugal and other countries, awakened the interest in the cultures of the "savages" or primitives: to know them better it could also be possible to control and exploit them better. In this way the ethnographic reports and the ethnology flourished, while the use of tools such as cameras and movie cameras allowed to document more and more accurately the customs and traditions of these people. Cultural anthropology collected all these contributions, inserting them in a wider context of analysis and scientific observation, thus becoming the "Science of Man".

Psychology instead comes into being in more recent times, from the rib of philosophy, always interested in man and his world, and from the theories of nineteenth-century psychiatry who were called in the beginning alienists, looked for the germs of the so-called "mental disease" rummaging in the brain and dedicated themselves to develop the most bizarre theories and therapeutic practices, depriving the patient of his personal dignity, reducing him to an object of study and segregating him in mental institutions.

In his work "Madness and Civilization: A History of Insanity in the Age of Reason", Michel Foucault analyzed the mechanisms of social marginalization and ghettoization reserved to the "insane" from the end of the Middle Ages onwards.

Psychology slowly gives back to the individual his quality of human being and recognizes in the symptoms produced by the mental disorder a particular language that has to be listened and interpreted to trace back the original causes.

Organicism in psychiatry that still sees today in the symptoms only an expression of an organic dysfunction, will continue to develop autonomously over time, by using various systems of treatment as electroshock, insulin coma, malarial therapy, lobotomy, cage beds, cold showers and also straitjackets.

Electroshock, a treatment that induces convulsion by making a powerful electrical discharge pass through the brain, was devised by the Italian neurologist Ugo Cerletti, after having attended the killing of some pigs in a slaughterhouse, previously stunned with a similar method.

The insulin coma therapy, also called deep sleep therapy, consisted of inducing an hypoglycemic coma in the patient in order to modify the mental functioning.

The malarial therapy was based on the assumption that the high fever caused by this disease could have a positive effect on the brain of the mentally ill persons; for this aim some Anopheles, carriers of the parasite, were bred in specific cages and used to infect the patients.

Lobotomy, devised at the end of the nineteenth century, was perfected in the forties and fifties by the doctors Walter Freeman and Antonio E. Moniz. The theory that supported this bloody practice was that the destruction of part of the prefrontal cerebral cortex of the patients would have eliminated many of their symptoms, making them more manageable. Moniz performed this operation by making some perforations in the brain, while Freeman in the United States developed a procedure that consisted in the insertion of a tool similar to an ice pick through the thin osseous tissue of the upper part of the orbit to reach the prefrontal cortex that was then partially destroyed with rapid movements. With this technique the doctor could perform dozens of operations per day on an outpatient basis. The result was often to reduce the patients to the condition of "zombies", as those efficiently shown in Milos Forman's "Someone Flew Over the Cuckoo's Nest".

Those listed above are some of the "remedies" used in the recent past to restrain patients that manifested behaviors or who where considered socially dangerous. In the meantime psychology, whose etymology indicates the study of the human soul and of the mind, from the second half of the nineteenth century onwards started slowly to earn the attribute "scientific" do to the fact that many scientists began to apply the methods of observation and experimentation used in natural science to study of the psyche. The psychology of conduct of Pierre Janet, the Soviet school of Pavlov and Vygotsky, the behaviorism of Skinner in the United States, the gestaltism in Germany and many others until the modern cognitive-behavioural approach and the attachment theory allowed this discipline to evolve, raising it to the rank of science and producing therapeutic methods of mental disorder based on protocols of psychotherapy corroborated by longitudinal and cross-cultural studies, along with the recent availability of drugs ever more effective and focused on the specific dysfunctions, with limited side effects.

This "egoistic" instinct of survival pushes us, as we have seen, to procure food, refuge and protection, therefore to seek security, and to find ways to mate and procreate in order to allow our genes to remain in the world. However, since the environment in which we live has limited resources and couldn't therefore allow everyone to easily achieve the goals mentioned above, we activate a competitive boost that brings us to compete for the best food (more probabilities of living long) and for the best partners (have many children in good health).

In the high-ranking animals, including us, this competition doesn't lead to the expulsion or the killing of the opponent, but to the establishment of a hierarchy with the mutual acknowledgement of the occupied rank. In due proportions, the above-mentioned laws are imposed upon all living species and each species has developed and preserved in the course of time their own specific strategies to ensure survival. These strategies can be defined, at least for all the vertebrates, as defense system, sexual or mating system and competitive and predatory system.

Contrary to the mating system that is activated only when the individual reaches sexual maturity, the defense and competitive systems are potentially active since birth. An infant cries and moves his head away from milk if it's too hot (defense) just as, in a litter of kittens, the most rugged and resourceful one pushes arrogantly the other away to attach first to the most milk wet nipple (competitiveness). Similarly, the push to procure food as response to the hunger stimulus activates, in many living species immediately after birth, the behaviors of predation. As we will analyze later, the human species is the only one that has developed the ability to act out predatory behaviors at the expense of individuals of the same species and to kill, torture and exterminate its own fellowmen. Whether the acquisition of this element is functional for the evolution laws or if it is an accidental mutation acquired and not eradicable, is still today a source of debate among geneticists.

In humans and anthropomorphic apes, in which the cerebral neocortex is present, a cooperative system has also developed and, when it is activated, it allows to build alliances and bonds between individuals to achieve a specific shared purpose. It is based on behaviors characterized by reciprocation (I help you be-

71

cause I expect that you do the same with me now or in the future) and by complicity (we want to achieve the same purpose and we have more possibilities of success if we ally).

To better understand how such ancient practices can become active in us and modulate in their expressions surpassing sometimes the filter of feelings and reason, we have to resort to the triune brain model developed by MacLean.*

MacLean individuated three regions of the human brain that retrace in broad terms in their structure the crucial phases of the evolution of our species. The deepest region of our brain is the one that responds to the individual primary needs, as survival and reproduction, and concerns the defense of the habitat, the search for food and the sexual impulse. In this region our primordial instincts originate, not mediated by the higher cerebral structures, and for this reason such region is called reptilian brain, shared with lower life forms of the evolution scale. The structure that overlaps it and that is present in all mammals is the limbic system. It's here that the emotions and the feelings that contribute to the construction of the social and emotional bonds and to the care giving of the offspring originate. The limbic system has an emotional memory, therefore preverbal, that stores the emotionally significant experiences as they are experienced by the individual in an exact moment both at a psychic and somatic level. We can define them in raw stage. Usually, the emotions accompanied by the corporeal sensations are elaborated by

*Paul D. MacLean, A Triune Concept of the Brain and Be-havior- 1973

the higher cerebral structures that give a meaning to the experience, storing it as a memory in a verbal form and therefore thinkable and tellable.

But sometimes traumatic events very intense and threatening may occur and arouse extreme defensive responses that, because of their nature, will not allow the elaboration and the memorization in form of memory, preventing the verbal explanation of the trauma to ourselves or to others. The events will re-main as if encapsulated in this traumatic memory and on specific environmental stimuli, emotions and so-matic sensations related to the experience of those events, even when they occurred far away in time, could re-emerge totally unexpected, intense and un-controllable, and above all incomprehensible because disconnected from the aforementioned events. This region of the brain is present, as we have said, in all mammals and gives proof to the belief of many re-searchers and of the majority of people with sensitivi-ty that animals also have emotions.

The latest evolutionary cerebral region, possessed by man and minimally by the anthropomorphic apes, chimpanzees and gorillas, is the neocortex or neopallium.   In it all the higher cognitive functions take place, from the language to the rational and ab-stract thought, to the explicit and declarative memory, not traumatic, and the moral sense. The impulses originated in the reptilian brain and the emotional baggage pertaining to the limbic system ar-rive to the neocortex where they are evaluated and

73

organized on the basis of the cognitions and analysis derived from the past experiences and of the current context indicators. Let's try to simplify what we have said: if we accidentally meet an individual of the other sex (or maybe of the same sex if we are homosexual) particularly attractive, the reptilian brain immediately generates sexual desire and the limbic system make us feel excited and troubled by this sudden attraction, and maybe even make us blush imperceptibly. Depending on the beliefs I have of me and on those of potential sexual partners, as well as on the past experiences, I could attempt an approach of some kind or desist. Obviously, the acquired ethical and moral conducts and the evaluation of the contextual circumstance will contribute to my decision.

In some cases, if the context assures me the impunity and the disclaimer for acts that are severely sanctioned in normal situations, as it happens in the actions of war or police repressions, violence up to murder, torture and rape against the "enemy" and women can be acted out directly, bypassing further mental processes.

Group violence and bullying also occur in this condition defined as "identity diffusion", a situation in which belonging to a group allows the individual to attenuate in it the personal responsibility and the awareness of his own individuality. To take part in a political demonstration, or to go to the stadium with other fans in support of the team, are also situations potentially able to degenerate into violent actions that a single isolated individual would probably never commit.

Fear

Fear is a primary emotion that comes from a response of the amygdale, a small area of the brain belonging to the limbic system, to a stimulus perceived as threatening and it is closely related to the instinct of survival. It aims to protect us from dangers, activating the system of defense. While for the majority of the living species the responses to danger situations are largely innate, in humans only some of them are, as fear of the dark or of sudden and violent noises which have protected us for millions of years from predators; while many other fears are acquired from birth. To show an example of innate fears, in a laboratory test a chick flees terrified if he is shown a glimpse of shadow made out of a cut out cardboard shaped as a bird of prey, even if he has never met one before in his life. So in the same manner a baby who crawls on a transparent surface, freezes up scared when he perceives a high step under the glass. But children learn very easily if a stimulus of any kind can be threatening or not for their safety, observing and understanding the emotional responses of their mother. If his mother is afraid, the child too will be frightened; if, instead, she smiles and shows herself calm, he will feel reassured. In the previous example, if the scared child sees his mother that urges him to keep going on the transparent surface and stretches her arms towards him while smiling, after a moment of hesitation he will continue his crawl on the transparent surface. Conversely, a mother frightened from the risk of contagious diseases and by dirty surfaces, to the point of cleaning obsessively door handles and windows nobs before touching them, could transmit her fear *to the* child. These are only a few simple examples but they illustrate efficaciously the mental mechanisms involved in the development of such a pervasive and powerful emotion.

We can assert that the primary need of every living being is the research of security and liberation from fear. The development of the neocortex and of the long-term memory has not only lead man to the perception of concrete and immediate dangers, but also to threatening situations feared or imagined as possible dangers in future time. Furthermore, to have suffered serious traumas in the past can lead to the massive reactivation of traumatic emotional responses even for the effectively neutral current situations that, for a certain perceptive element, are associated with the suffered trauma.

A woman raped by her father since the age of five, once adult succeeded, with much difficulty, in creating her own family and in having a sufficiently normal sex life but during and after the coitus every time she needed to execute specific rituals and behaviors in order to avoid perceiving the smell of sperm since the olfactory stimulus, dramatically reactivated traumatic memories of the abuses suffered during childhood, even after many years.

But when can an event be defined as traumatic? What characterizes a trauma? We can answer that basically the conditions are two: to perceive the situation as a threat to our physical safety to the point of

77

fearing of being killed, and to feel totally powerless to defend ourselves. This last point, that is the condition of total powerlessness, is the key marker that always characterizes a trauma. In this regard, the tortures executed by the Inquisition on their victims or of those prisoners in the concentration camps is the image that comes immediately to mind; but also the physical and sexual abuse acted against a child or a gang rape on a teenager girl causes the same effects on the victim's psyche. Furthermore, we can define a trauma on the base of its permanence in time. In psychology we define Traumas with a capital T, the events that happened only once and for a short time, just as an assault, a mourning or a car accident; and with a lower-case t, but not for this less serious, the ones that continued over time, for example throughout the childhood, suffered within a significant bond.

At the end of the nineteenth century, some researchers, among whom Pierre Janet in France, began to study the effects of childhood traumas on the lives of individuals, highlighting a clear relationship between the experiences lived during childhood and the mental disorders, at that time called hysteria or neurosis, observed in adults. Pierre Janet, decades in advance, revealed the close connection between traumatic memories and the dissociation, meant as a mechanism of defense from the powerful emotions and feelings associated with the trauma. Freud too seemed to realize the causal link between childhood abuses and mistreatment and the hysterical condition manifested by his patients. Jeffrey M. Masson, editor of the Freudian archives and Anna Freud's collaborator, in his book *The Assault on Truth* writes:

" In 1895 and 1896 Freud, in listening to his women patients, learned that something dreadful and violent lay in their past. The psychiatrists who had heard these stories before Freud had accused their patients of being hysterical liars and had dismissed their memories as fantasy. Freud was the first psychiatrist who believed his patients were telling the truth. These women were sick, not because they came from "tainted" families, but because something terrible and secret had occurred to them as children. Freud announced his discovery in a paper which he gave in April 1896 to the Society for Psychiatry and Neurology in Vienna, his first major public address to his peers."

Unfortunately, after few years, Freud, maybe dismayed by the hostile reactions raised in the medical environment by his researches, renounced to carry on his first intuition claiming that the traumatic memories that emerged from the subconscious, that is from the dissociated parts of the self according to Janet, were only incestuous fantasies of little girls and boys towards the parent of the opposite sex.

Today traumatology has instead confirmed the devastating effect that the traumatic experiences, suffered during the developmental age, have on people's lives.

Statistical researches, carried out in different European countries and in the United States, have revealed that 15-30 percent of a sample of adult women interviewed, had suffered abuses and mistreatments or harassments during childhood. However, considering the reticence that certain kinds of questions raise during the interviews, it is supposed that the percentages are even higher. Often these repeated traumas were accompanied by emotional abuses and carelessness from the mothers who, in any case, had neither protected nor believed them. In recent years traumatology has finally acquired the primary role in the comprehension of the development of psychic and somatic pathologies in human subjects who were abused or seriously neglected during childhood and adolescence. The symptoms arising from the exposure to a traumatic event are defined as PTSD, Post Traumatic Stress Disorder, and the most important of them is the impairment of the ability to realistically assess whether the situations in which we find ourselves are safe or threatening. The perception of the present is distorted by the consequences of past traumas.

In the field of the psychotherapeutic treatment of the post-traumatic stress disorders, a method of intervention has been developed by the researcher Francine Shapiro. It is based on the bilateral stimulation of the brain through the ocular movements and is called EMDR (Eye Movement Desensitization and Reprocessing). This method gives excellent results, allowing the re-emergence of the dissociated traumatic memories and their successive processing and modification. Every bilateral stimulation, right and left, made by moving the eyes or perceiving the tactile sensations, seems to facilitate the relaxation inhibiting the sympathetic nervous system and then by reducing anxious response. The effectiveness of this kind of treatment had already been grasped by those who practiced hypnosis with the method of the pendulum and by practicing some yoga techniques. We all know the relaxing power of the bilateral swinging practiced by mothers who hold their child in their arms to the point of reproducing it with cradles and once adult, with hammocks.

To conclude this short description on traumas, we can affirm that the genetic makeup and the type of attachment developed during childhood prepare ourselves to face more or less effectively the stressful events of life, ability that in clinical jargon is called resilience. Nevertheless, these events will in any case influence our personal development as much as to say that "we are our past".

The defense system

The fear deriving from a danger situation, real or imagined, always activates in humans the defense system. It has the function of defending us from the external dangers allowing us to react and to not succumb. A really powerful stimulus able to activate this system is the awareness of being in danger, alone and with no certainty of receiving help.

To have a family and belong to a social group increases the sense of personal security and self-confidence allowing to deal more effectively with the threats to our safety. The family is the first social nucleus in human history and can assume, as de facto it did, very different forms in the various cultures and human groups. In contrast to popular belief, it is not limited to only monogamous couple, since the anthropologists have provided documentary evidences of many forms of polygyny (a man married to more than one woman) and some forms of polyandry (a woman married to more that one man, usually two or more brothers). But the main function of any matrimonial institution has been, and in much of the world still is, that of forming alliances between human groups, families, tribes, clans or, in more recent history, nations. To exchange gifts or exchange women has always been the means used by men to strengthen their social or family group and thus to increase their feeling of collective security. This probably helps to better understand the meaning of the last two commandments of the ten listed in the Bible according to the

Catholic Church: You shall not covet your neighbor's wife; You shall not covet your neighbor's goods.

In any case, since the beginning of human history, to stay alone has always meant for the majority of the individuals to meet early death. The prehistoric man who after an exhausting hunting returned exhausted and empty-handed to his refuge, if he could count on a lit fire and on a hot soup made with herbs, tubers and roots previously picked by his mate and on the solidarity of his group, had statistically more probabilities not to get sick or not to die from starvation. The woman, on her part, couldn't have guaranteed for herself and her children any hope of survival if she couldn't count on the material help of her own man and clan.

The expulsion from the community (ostracism) was considered in the past one of the harshest punishments for crimes committed against society, as for example the infraction of a taboo, because it sanctioned the isolation and often the consequent death for stress of the guilty person. The abandonment experience, the conviction of being left alone in the world and exposed to any predator or enemy that acts in the dark, are the most powerful and oldest stimulants of our defense system. To still feel uneasiness or fear when we remain alone in the dark, even as adults, shouldn't be considered a neurotic irrational phobia or a childish feeling but the survival over time of an extremely adaptive behavioral response that has allowed us to successfully overcome the dangers and the difficulties of an often dramatically hostile environmental context. Our current highly technological civilization has eliminated or extremely reduced the dangers deriving from possible predators and at least for most of us, has freed us from the primary needs, assuring availability of food, shelter and warmth; but hasn't freed us from fear and anxiety, paradoxically allowing our uncertainties to increase, as it is proved by the ever wider recourse of psychiatric drugs by so many people in western countries. Living alone, as proven by many researchers, in fact, is still a source of stress and creates a predisposition to diseases and accidents in respect to individuals who live in a family or in a community.

The defense system pertains to some deep nuclei of the brain, the brainstem and vagus nerve, that is the autonomic nervous system, and includes the immune system. We can omit to analyze in detail the physiology, too complicated for this field, and we can focus on the somatic, psychic and behavioral effects that derive from its activation.

The autonomic nervous system (ANS) has always been described as consisting of two opposed and antagonistic subsystems, called sympathetic and parasympathetic. The synergy of these two systems modulates the emotions and the corporeal sensations, making us feel fear, anxiety, fulfillment or pleasure. However, researches in recent years, especially those carried out by the neuroscientist Stephen Porges, have redefined the role of ANS, no longer as an interaction between two antagonistic subsystems, with the prevalence of either depending on the circumstances in which we are, but as a hierarchical structure that characterizes a system of defense, physiologically very complex, that proceeds by degrees from top to bottom. The highest level corresponds to the sensation of a state of security that predisposes us to calm and to social interaction. It makes us curious and exploratory and strongly connects us to reality. The perception or the concrete presence of a threat for our safety activates instead the underlying levels which function is to enable us to defend ourselves as effectively as possible and to neutralize the danger.

Three levels of activation of the defense system have been described and defined, even in their physiological and neurological correlatives. They are called in clinical jargon "the four f": *fight and flee, freeze* and *faint*.

The first level - fight and flee - is evolutionarily the most complex because it entails the immediate and accurate evaluation of the circumstance we have to face and the consequent decision to attack to defend ourselves and try to prevail or to escape as quickly as possible to move away from danger. In the case of a fight against an aggressor it's also necessary to know how to interpret the signals sent by the other individual, in addition to the information that we receive from our body, to put an end within a reasonable time to the conflict, triumphing on the rival or submitting to him and recognizing thus his superiority. This entails the processing in the cerebral neocortex of the signals that come from the deepest levels of the brain. So, we can consider this manner of reaction as the most evolved, mainly because it involves the retention of the relationship with the other even during competition or aggression.

85

The activation of the defense system at this level is modulated in intensity by the contextual and relational information that we receive: initially we approach with caution a stranger because he could be threatening, or we find ourselves anxious because we are in a social situation over which we have no control. The recognition of specific signals, verbal and non-verbal, (greeting, smile, friendly attitude, or hostile attitude, clenched jaw, etc.) will put an end to the sequence of maneuvers and defensive preliminaries, or will prepare the organism to a more effective defense. When it is activated, the effects on the visceral system, more or less intense depending on the different situations, are acceleration of the heartbeat, contraction of stomach muscles, shortness of breath, digestion arrest and intestinal peristalsis; the blood flows to the voluntary muscles at the expense of the internal organs. The individual is ready to escape or fight. The limbic system allows us to feel the emotions of anger and/or fear.

The second level - freeze - entails the massive activation of the adrenergic sympathetic system and can be defined as a state of "alarmed suspension" of every activity: the hypertonia of the voluntary muscular system freeze us in the situation and in the position in which we are; the visceral system halts. This level is activated when the higher level is "skipped", bypassed for excess load, as when we are in the presence of a sudden, unpredictable and potentially mortal danger and prepares the intervention of the last level to implement a possible extreme defense.

An unbearable trauma, perceived as the loss of all hope of salvation, leads to the activation of the third level (faint) that determines the collapse of the whole organism and "apparent death": it's the so-called "vasovagal reaction" that in the extreme cases can lead to cardiac arrest. However, this defense mechanism, probably the most archaic because originally developed in fishes and amphibians, can in some cases save our life. The prey that falls down as dead before the predator can, indeed, persuade it to end its attack, maybe to look around in search of a safe place to withdraw and to make sure that there aren't in the vicinity other predators that could compete; those few seconds could be enough for the prey to escape rapidly, suddenly recovering all its strength. The activation of these last two levels entails emotional weakening, closure in themselves and withdrawal from reality up to dissociation. For this reason every possibility of relationship and interaction is inhibited.

This hierarchy of the defense system allows the organism to modulate the response depending on the seriousness of the danger that threatens us: to feel attacked by the vexation of a bulling boss or being attacked by a furious Rottweiler, ultimately should not be perceived as the same thing. But exactly the incongruous activation in respect to the real event of the above described levels and/or the excessive and sometimes chronic persistence of this activation, without the consequent deactivation when the danger has ceased, can cause many psychological problems and a lot of suffering. To better explain, the devastating pain of a prisoner in a concentration camp or that of a child seriously mistreated by his own parent, will activate a system of defense with the most congruous manners in respect to the situation and this will be functional in order to increase their probabilities of staying alive. On the contrary, an individual subject to a sudden panic attack without a real and concrete external danger, will experience in any case an uncontrollable distress of death, due to the massive but incongruous activation of the above-mentioned system. Even being in a new situation, never experienced before, as traveling to a foreign country culturally very different from our own, could trigger improperly the defense system if this difference is interpreted as potentially threatening. This circumstance has been called cultural shock. The incongruous or chronic activation of the defense system, just as the generalized anxiety or the panic attacks in situation that realistically pose no danger, suggests the event of serious traumas suffered in the past and not yet resolved.

The competitiveness.

Within phylogenetic tree, that is the evolutionary path that goes from the most elementary forms of life to the most complex ones, the competitive system appears, from the bottom up, as pure defense of the territory and living space, as well as predation against other species to get food; in the fight against other subjects of the same species, the loser must leave or risks to be killed. Starting from rats up, the competitive system is structured in two poles of dominance and submission that allows the creation of hierarchical and cohesive social systems based on the rank. The fight ends when one of the two competitors declares himself to be defeated by acting out a behavior that expresses the acknowledgement of the winner's superiority, for example, exposing a vulnerable part of his body as the stomach, or by taking on the position of the female of the species when she offers herself for mating. In this manner the animal acknowledges the dominant role of the winner (alpha individual) but accepting this hierarchical position, he isn't forced to leave the territory and will continue to be part of the group. The evolutionary leap that led to this type of competition is due to the acquisition of new memory capabilities that enable the *recognition* of the relational quality Self-Other.

Most birds don't recognize their own eggs, even if they brood them; this allows the cuckoo to throw away with impunity from the nest the eggs laid by the

89

legitimate owner, replacing them with its own, often bigger in size more than double. Fishes and amphibians usually lay their eggs in the surrounding environment or in precisely chosen places, leaving them to their fate. The evolutionary acquisition of this new ability instead, allows recognition of the offspring, in order to be able to take care of it efficiently until they achieve complete autonomy and it also intervenes, as we will see, in mating to form a stable couple. The lack of recognition of the offspring leads therefore to a reproductive strategy based on a very high number of eggs laid; even if only a small percentage of these will escape predators, those survivors will still be sufficient for the conservation of the species. Conversely, the acquisition of the recognition allows to restrict to few units the number of offsprings because it can be effectively cared-for and protected up to adulthood; similarly, it allows the establishment of hierarchies based on dominance between individuals of the same group. Chimpanzees aggregate in social groups divided into different levels of rank, each one characterized by particular privileges and priorities for access of food and females; levels that are often contested and redefined by fierce conflicts between males of the group, without ever killing voluntarily the rival.

The competitive system, once activated to define the rank, must in any case be deactivated in a short time, by coming quickly to a satisfying solution for the two contenders. In fact, our endocrine system can't be kept permanently under pressure by the competitive system and the constant activation of the latter (stalemate) is a cause of great stress and can lead in some cases even to death. This has been verified with tests on animals where the competition for the territory normally determines the expulsion of the loser: if the defeated animal is placed in a cage next to the winner, thus preventing him to leave after the fight, and therefore can't deactivate his competitive system by fleeing, consequently he dies from stress.

Many ethnologists and anthropologists have reported, in their observations on human groups studied, how a curse or an "evil eye", pronounced by the shaman or the village head (alpha individuals) against another individual, often caused death from stress, if he didn't find an efficient antidote capable of putting an end to his competitive stalemate.

To compete with other species to defend our own vital space and to compete within our own species to gain a dominant hierarchical position is therefore part of the laws of evolution. But the human species, has developed in the course of hundreds of thousands years the ability to build and use tools to increase the efficacy in the fight for survival and supremacy; tools that, starting from a femur used as a club (masterfully displayed by the director Stanley Kubrik in his film "2001: A Space Odyssey") became, however, over time the bearers of an immense destructive potential. The last two world wars, with tens of millions of casualties among soldiers and civilians, and the current capability to inflict huge losses to the "enemy" minimizing the risks by means of radio-controlled weapons such as drones, have amply demonstrated it.

However, the technological development hasn't been accompanied by an analogous progress of the human soul; the patents that, for mere profits, impede that everyone can use the conquests of medicine and engineering, or the exploitation of the human and natural resources of people on other people are only an example that highlights how the need for dominance is still a priority among the motivations that push our species.

Unfortunately, another specific trait acquired exclusively by humans, namely to act out predatory behaviors aimed at killing not only at the expense of other living species but also between individuals of the same species; man can become a sadistic killer of his fellows, as our history teaches us, making dramatically real the Latin saying, taken over time by many thinkers, "Homo homini lupus", that is "man as predator of other men". This happens by depriving the victim of his human identity and dignity, alienating him and treating him as an object of predation. Slavery, torture, genocide and exploitation of women and children are unfortunately still valid examples of what has been said. The strategy of the major multinational corporations to make use of the manpower enlisted in the countries of the so-called Third World, underpaid and forced to work in highly dangerous and humiliating conditions, indeed inhuman, is a present example of it.

At the time of the so-called "discovery" of America the natives were considered subhuman and treated like animals and in a few decades, with the alibi of civilization and evangelization, the extermination of tens of millions of individuals and the destruction of highly evolved cultures took place. Many years passed before a Pope, Paul III, affirmed that the inhabitants of the New World were endowed with a soul like everyone, even if they were in any case savages and so subject by nature to submit to the cruel "protection" of the civilized conquerors.

The extended development of the neocortex has allowed ourselves to be place at the vertex of the evolutionary ladder, enabling us to build increasingly perfected and effective tools to dominate and change the environment for our exclusive benefit, and by making us even capable of imagining the future. However, this last capability turned out to be a double-edged sword.

The fight for hierarchy and for the conservation of the positions of power in the non-human primates never lead to the voluntary killing of the defeated enemy, least of all to the destruction of its habitat; the conflict ends with the recognition of the hegemonic position of the winner (individual or group), and of the subordinate one of the loser.

The Bonobos, a kind of small chimpanzees living in a narrow equatorial area of Africa and studied for a long time by the primatologist Frans de Waal, have found a very nice way to regulate and terminate every conflict between themselves: the use sexual gratification. Their behavior seems to remember the famous slogan in vogue during the seventies: Make love, not war! Their females, similarly to human females, are not subject to oestrus and are sexually active all the year round.

Furthermore, they mate face to face, in the so-called missionary position, and don't disdain from oral and anal sex, masturbation and homosexuality.

The peculiar human capability to prefigure future events, combined with the struggle to gain and maintain the dominance positions, has made it possible to imagine the enemy defeated today as a probable enemy tomorrow, maybe even stronger and more motivated by the spirit of revenge. So, it is necessary to eliminate him, destroy him and to eliminate and destroy also his children and grandchildren that might one day avenge him. This assumption has been proven by the fratricidal fights that have always characterized the climb to the positions of power and by the stories of all the wars of conquest, starting from those told in the Old Testament in which Moses scolds his generals after a battle because they had spared too many civilians: *"Now therefore, kill every male among the little ones, and kill every woman who has known man by lying with him. But all the young girls who have not known man by lying with him keep alive for yourself".* (Numbers 31:1-18)

To imagine even our own children as possible competitors for the rank or as potential dangers for our own safety and to arrive for this reason to physically eliminate them, is also an event many times reported in the myths of many populations and dramatically confirmed in the course of human history.

In conclusion, in the relationships between individuals, the competitive system is always the one that is activated first when it is necessary to establish the reciprocal hierarchical positions and to master every new relational situation.

Another system, pertaining to human species denominated cooperative has been identified and works as a social glue more or less temporary to form an alliance, a partnership, a group on the basis of sharing and of cooperation that are, often aimed to a project of dominance on other alliances, partnerships and groups. This certainly happens in all team games, from football to bridge and in all wars.

Some reflections on dominance yet.

"To be a normal person consists, first of all, in succeeding in remaining normal in respect to ourselves and not to the majority, intended as a social system subject to judgements of values aimed to control and functional dominance. It is necessary, for this reason, to reserve the possibility to act according to our impulses, coherently to our desires. (...) But the space, in which this action is carried out, is also occupied by others. It is essential to avoid the conflict because from it will necessarily arise a hierarchical scale of dominance that alienates our own desire to the desire of others. On the other hand, to submit ourselves means to accept, with the submission, the psychosomatic pathology that derives inevitably from the impossibility to act according to our own impulses. To rebel is not the solution: because if the rebellion is made by a group it is called revolution and soon reconstitutes a hierarchical scale of submission within the group itself, whereas the solitary rebellion or deviance brings rapidly to the suppression or alienation of the rebel from the abnormal generality that consid-

95

ers itself, for purely quantitative merits, holder of normality. All that remains is escape."

These words from the biologist and researcher Henri Laborit, define the problem of the continuous research of dominance in the relationships between individuals of a social group and express his solution, just as the author identifies it.

Laborit doesn't mean with "escape" the escape from the world and its laws, or at least not only that, but he indicates the unique way to avoid an unsolvable competitive situation, a competitive stalemate, that would activate the neurological system of the inhibition of action (corresponding with freeze or faint, to recall the previously described strategies of the defense system) that, if not deactivated in a short time, would lead us to get sick or worse, to die. Mobbing in workplaces and bullying so frequent in schools and in the armed forces are indeed situations of competitive stalemate from which the victim doesn't succeed in freeing himself and for which an immediate solution is neither expected nor allowed; their effects on physical and psychic health are devastating. A rather common example of competitive stalemate could be a latent conflict between an employee of a company and his office manager, when the latter doesn't hold his position for a recognized merit. The impossibility of the employee to recognize a real leadership in his superior, who is incompetent but strongly recommended, at the same time does not give him the possibility to act out a strategy of "attack" without risking to be denounced for aggression or even yet dismissed, poses the relationship between the two in a competitive stalemate. In this case, if it isn't possible to act out the strategy of "escape" by presenting a job resignation, it is, however, possible to use a mental escape, a sort of controlled dissociation in which the individual can say to himself: "My body is obliged to stay here but I can be elsewhere with my mind." This mechanism of mental escape can be in some cases the only possible defense from a situation that threats our psychophysical safety and in which all the other strategies turn out to be inadequate.

In man's history some examples of escape from the world are those of the hermit monks, withdrawn in inaccessible places as the stylites who lived perched on a column or, nowadays, of the hobos or homeless persons who voluntarily have chosen to retire from society and its laws. But it is anyway very difficult, if not impossible, to escape the demon of dominance. Everywhere a human group is created, the push for dominance emerges powerful; a group of monks, united by the same Creed and withdrawn in an isolated monastery on top of a mountain after some time can't escape the need to gain power internally and damage the human community they belong to. Umberto Eco in his novel "Nel nome Della Rosa" and Aldous Huxley in "The Devils of Loudun" describe in detail these complicated dynamics, that torment their protagonists.

How this compulsion of dominance is permanently assimilated and not eradicable is demonstrated by our history that tells how every time an individual or a subordinate group has succeeded in gaining the power in the name of justice and equality, has after inexorably changed from oppressed to oppressor, from victim to persecutor. The "happy nonexistent place", that is the island of Utopia described by Sir Thomas More, is indeed an ideal society where cooperation and solidarity rule and where, just as in the utopian socialism, everyone obtains according to his needs and offers in accordance to his possibilities. However, reality turned out to be very different: even a person who dedicates his own life to others, without realizing it, responds to a need of feeling better and thus higher or, in other cases, of humiliating himself and being relegated among the last, hoping in any case to be among the first in an hypothetical other life, as promised by Jesus in the Sermon on the Mount. So, it's very easy to be charitable or lavish donations; it's very difficult instead to act according to the principle of solidarity and of equal rights, as failure of the socialistic and communist ideas in the world and the triumph of a global capitalism resembling dramatically to a ruthless social darwinism have largely demonstrated.

Similarly to the Marxian theory of the transformation of money as object of exchange to obtain goods to the money becoming merchandise in itself, the same happens in the case of dominance, transformed from a tool to obtain the priority in the access to the environmental resources to the greedy and unlimited pursuit of idle power in itself. Since the existence of human society organized in hierarchical structures, priests, pharaohs, kings and emperors, in other words, clergy and the nobility always assisted by the caste of warriors, have squandered immense human and material resources for the sole purpose of exhibiting their self-proclaimed superiority, often elevated to the rank of gods or demigods. Pyramids, mausoleums, royal and imperial palaces, castles, cathedrals and more, nowadays show mercilessly in their magnificence, how the mere idea of equality and of fair distribution of the resources among human beings is unrealistic since it is counterposed to the miserable existence of being compelled by force or persuaded by a promise of reward in another life, to build them.

The religious thought, born from the need of transcendence, that is to believe that another reality, fairer and more comprehensible than this in which we live, is conceivable and also possible, has produced, very efficiently, some systems of beliefs, myths and religions, coherent and functional to the needs of the different human societies that have created them.

Some indigenous populations of South America, decimated by the colonization and deprived of their lands and all their resources, elaborated, at the end of the nineteenth century, a religion based on the endlessly peregrination in the Amazonian forest in search for a sort of promised land, called the Land-without-Evil, where the Spanish and Portuguese conquerors would have disappeared into and that there would have been food and security for everyone. Similarly, more recently, other indigenous populations, threatened and driven to starvation by the deforestation and the imposition of one-crops farming practiced by the multinational corporations, developed a religious systems in which the airplanes of the white man would have landed one day near their villages, on dirt

99

tracks expressly built by them, to bring them every-thing they needed (*Cargo Cult*). These examples illus-trate the desperate search for a way out of the hor-rors of colonization, implemented by the people who have been within a short time violently deprived of the lands on which they have always lived in and of their freedom. The unintelligible and unbearable reali-ty could then be overcome with the recourse of these new myths, called millenarianisms for the analogy with the year one thousand of the Christian era, in which the end of the times and the imminent advent of a Messiah, capable of creating "another" world where there would have been peace, prosperity and justice for everyone, were expected. The intolerable and cruel dominion of the Roman Empire on the an-cient Palestine, started in 63 BC, led the Jews to ex-pect the advent of a Messiah to come and free them from slavery and to restore the Kingdom of David; while in medieval Europe, devastated by invasions, famines and diseases, everyone expected the end of the year one thousand with the arrival of the Kingdom of Christ.

It isn't possible to free ourselves from the need of building hierarchies depending on the rank. The East-ern religions, such as Hinduism and Buddhism, even if they appear to be more mystical, contemplative and redeeming than the others, they too define, for ex-ample with the hateful castes system or the progres-sive ascent toward the Revelation according to the different acquired merits, a strict hierarchical scale of values.

Christianity and Islamism, derived both from Judaism and just as the latter strictly structured in hierarchies, are currently the most common revealed (namely characterized by holy books that contain the word of God revealed directly to his prophets) are the most spread religions. To attest their Faith they have uprooted with violence every residual form of paganism and every form of deviance from orthodoxy and then they have fought against each other for centuries (and even now some fundamentalist Islamic fringes lead a Holy War) not because they want to impose on the World the only true God, as they claim, but because they actually justify and legitimize all the strategies aimed at the domain and control of the human and material resources of the planet. The "afterworld" itself, professed by them, meticulously reflects the hierarchical structure of society; in the presence of God, there are the Angels, Archangels, Seraphs, Cherubs, Thrones and further below are the Devils, Archdevils and so on, as Dante Alighieri has poetically and meticulously illustrated in his Divine Comedy.

Since the existence of organized human groups in our society, dominance and social control have always been pursued and have kept individuals subordinate through the two most powerful emotions ascribable to the competitive system, *shame* and *fear,* using concrete threats, as those of torture and stakes, or abstract but maybe more effective as the condemnation to Hell or Gehenna in the judgement day, that dreaded "Dies Irae", the day of the rage, when the Lord, as we were taught as children, will not be very benevolent with us ("...*Many are called, but few are chosen*", Matthew 20:1-16)

In conclusion, we could summarize what we have said until now, positioning the human action in two big classes of behaviors, borrowing and re-elaborating the last Freudian theory in order of time based on two opposing impulses present in human soul, called *libido* and *mortido*. In the first one we can put all the activities aimed at building the bonds designed for the conservation of the individual and the species, such as mating, attachment, caregiving, defense system, and also cooperation and altruism (libido or impulse of life), whereas the other gathers the strategies aimed at gaining the control and the power on the environment and our fellows (mortido or impulse of death). Libido builds bonds and so is creative; love for life, art and creativity in general belong to it. Mortido destroys them; violence, abuse of power and war belong to it. So, the ancient dualism between Eros and Thanatos, originally postulated by Empedocles and reformulated by Freud, would be dramatically confirmed.

Yet some considerations on the altruism motivation.

This predisposition, already present in anthropomorphic apes such as chimpanzees and gorillas, is fully developed only in human species. When it is activated, it uses the typical signals of a communication between compeers as "I don't want to attack you to compete" and one of these signal can be a smile, a game or the shared curiosity for an object. The activation of the cooperative system always puts an end to the conflicts for the rank and promotes friendship, alliance and sharing. We might then consider the drive to collaboration as the effect of a momentary deactivation of the competitive system that allows the emergence of more advanced and functional strategies for our species in view of a socially useful purpose or goal. The deactivation of the competitive system allows also to implement behaviors of solidarity and help towards suffering or life-threatening individuals. Also this altruistic drive although it is difficult to believe, is functional to the survival of the species and is inscribed in our DNA; in effect it may not appear favorable to the survival of the individual when the latter sacrifices himself for others, but is in any case functional to the survival of his genes. The researchers W.D. Hamilton and G. Price developed in the sixties an interesting mathematical equation to prove this assumption. Intuitively, we can easily understand how the sacrifice of a mother for her children is adaptive for the perpetuation of her own genes, and how the concept of reciprocation can justify the generalized altruism; what I do for you today, I expect someone else to do for me tomorrow. The sacred character of hospitality that in all the human cultures imposed to accept, without conditions refugees, wayfarers or fugitives, came about exactly from this need.

In the technologically advanced and complex society in which we live in today these needs of solidarity and cooperation seem obsolete, and instead exalts in self-sufficiency, aggression and competition, devaluing the emotional needs, fundamental for our security, and our well-being. These needs, however, will inevitably resume the upper hand every time that we experience loneliness, illness, insecurity and fear. The missed satisfaction of these needs could be perceived, in the current highly competitive social context, as a personal defeat, leading the individual to experience a feeling of shame and humiliation, sentencing him to depression or, worse, to react with aggressive behaviors towards his last battle not to succumb.

Emotions.

Normally, in everyday language, emotions and feelings take on similar meanings. Actually, we can define a feeling as a conscious and prolonged emotional state, not necessarily in connection with another individual. In fact, just as we can feel love or affection for a loved one, a friend or our pet, present or distant in time, we can experience an isolated feeling that can be brief and very intense as the one that seized Stendhal in Florence before the painting of the Mona Lisa of Leonardo, or more diluted over time as a sunset by the sea. So, what distinguishes feelings from emotions is the duration over time and the greater awareness of their origin. Love, hatred, nostalgia, contempt are defined feelings. Pleasure, anger, sadness and disgust could be the correlated emotions. A feeling is born and preserved, often jealously, in the depths of our heart; an emotion instead is something that demands an immediate conceived or acted response.

Emotions originates in specific areas of the brain and are correlated with inputs both physiological, as fear when we experience a sudden intense pain, and psychological, such as the rage that sometimes we experience when we think back to a person who has hurt us. Emotions usually, predispose the body to act and inform the others of our frame of mind; therefore they exercise a strong communicative function that expresses itself through body language (facial and postural expressions). This communicative function can sometimes influence others, making them feel the same emotions for empathy; this phenomenon occurs regularly every time we are intensely captivated, when we attend a theatrical or cinematographic show, and is due to the activation of the so-called mirror neurons in our brain. These cerebral cells, identified a few years ago with the neuroimaging technique, are activated when attending as spectators an event of high emotional impact, we feel really involved as if we where directly taking part in it.

The communicative function of our emotions is made possible by the physiological alterations that occur in our body (blushing that appears on our face when we feel embarrassment or shame, or the tears of sorrow or joy that streams down our cheeks) and by the facial and postural signals correlated with them, such as those indicating contempt and anger that, intentionally heightened, are used in martial arts to intimidate enemies. The defiance dance of the Maori, called Haka, practiced by the rugby team All Blacks of New Zealand and of which the communicative effectiveness is immediately obvious to anyone who follows this sport, explains this function exactly.

The corporeal function involved in the emotions are those linked with the cardiovascular system (heart rate, blood pressure), electrodermal conductivity (perspiration, salivation), respiratory rate (breathlessness), pupil's diameter, variation in body temperature and muscular hypertonia (tension, muscles contraction). The operation of "lie detector" machines is based upon the measurement of the variations of corporeal parameters compared to the normal state

106

and on the observation of facial expressions. We can very well see examples of this in many American series such as "Lie to Me" or "Criminal Minds".

The anthropologist Desmond Morris has long studied "body language" confirming how the communicative signals caused by emotions are universally present and identical in all populations of the Earth.

We affirmed that the emotions have mainly a communicative function because they always imply a real or fantasized interaction with the other; so we can now list and better analyze them attributing them to the different motivational systems that we have illustrated earlier. To feel emotions is inevitable, because they are a physiological and adaptive response in certain life situations. What may change from person to person is the way we manage them, passing from one extreme where they are perceived intense and uncontrollable, as it occurs for example in panic attacks or anger fits, to the other extreme where they are instead blocked and denied upon onset, or more rarely, completely separated from consciousness. What characterizes the individuals who suffer from the so-called borderline personality disorder, is exactly the scarce or the unability to stop and take time to reflect on the emotions, usually perceived intensely, or even to think about them, going instead straight to act the correlated behaviors, called *acting out* and becoming often dangerous to oneself and to others. Conversely, an adult who learned from childhood, not to express certain emotions such as anger and hostility, connoted as negative and maybe harshly punished, will have learned to repress them to the point of not being aware of them. But his emotional world, even if so detached from consciousness, will seek in any case a way to express itself, and will do it through the body; through specific psychosomatic disorders.

Let's identify now which are the emotions that can be attributed to the activation of the attachment.

The emotion linked to separation anxiety and fear, resulting from a real or dreaded threat of abandonment is certainly one. We have sees how abandonment, to find ourselves alone, is always perceived as a danger for our safety, to which finds a solution only the certainty that the separation from the people that love and take care of us will be temporarily. For this reason, the child who will face his first day of nursery school, among unknown teachers and children, will initially complain and cry, but if he has build a secure attachment he will soon calm down, confident that his mother hasn't left him in a dangerous situation and will return to pick him up as promised.

The *separation anger,* the *protest* and the *anger* for abandonment or the loss of a loved one, followed by *despair* and grief when we become aware that this person won't come back, are always attributable to the attachment system. These are followed by the *emotional detachment* and the reorganization of our life when we overcome the mourning. When the need of reassurance is promptly satisfied, we obviously feel *happiness* and a *sensation of security*.

The emotions arising by the activation of the competitive system are, anxiety and fear deriving from expectations of assessment and judgement or from threats to our physical safety, *anger* of challenge, the desire for revenge, but also *sadness*, caused by a defeat suffered in a competition. While anxiety, fear and anger are common to the different motivational systems, shame and humiliation belong purposely to the competitive system and are related to the recognition of the other's superiority. The blushing that often accompanies, at a somatic level, is due to deactivation at the end of the competitive activation: the blood flows back from the muscular and visceral apparatus, that was prepared to fight, to the peripheral flow of the body.

To perceive ourselves defeated, as well as sad and suffering, for the loss of an emotional bond because of a separation or a divorce, introduces a competitive element in the experience of abandonment that predisposes to resentment and can lead to self-destructive behaviors and to cultivate dangerous desires of retaliation and revenge.

When we win a competition, we feel, instead, *pride* and a *sensation of triumph*. *Envy* arises and strengthens when the competitive system is always active even if latent, leading the individual to perceive himself inept and a loser in a specific interaction with others. When it becomes pervasive, it can easily turn into *self-contempt*.

Also the courtship and behaviors aimed at mating are usually accompanied by specific emotions of which the best known is *anxiety* related to a possible rejection of the sexual approach. The performance anxiety that affects mainly men, is instead attributed to the competitive system and should be precisely redefined as evaluation anxiety, often independent of a real judgmental behavior of the partner and attributable to feelings of worthlessness of which men are only partially aware. The *desire* to have only for ourselves our partner and the *jealousy*, as well as *modesty*, are additional emotions pertaining to sexual motivation.

We have seen that the attachment is closely related to the complementary caregiving system. *Tenderness* is the emotion aroused by the request of caregiving signaled by the other. For this reason every little small being, human or animal "inspires tenderness". It has been proven that this emotion is correlated with the increased presence of a specific hormone oxytocin in the bloodstream.

When we are afraid we have missed a caregiving request, as well when we are convinced of not being a good mother, we feel a specific sense of guilt, of not being suitable, capable or, to quote the psychoanalyst Winnicot, of not being a sufficiently good parent. Not being able to calm the cries of her own child can become for some mothers, a serious reason of self-incrimination and cause distressing emotions of *inadequacy*. Another typical emotion of caregiving is sadness in the separations, that usually precedes the deactivation of this system. Such is the sadness, that parents experience when their children reach independence and leave home, a situation defined as the empty nest syndrome, even if it is disguised by satisfaction and maybe even pride. The last one is the *educational anger*, not to be confused with mistreatment and punishments. Such is the reproach or the spanking of the child when his behavior risks to put him in a dangerous situation, such as prevent him from putting his fingers in the electrical sockets or from touching the gas stove knobs.

Loyalty and sense of belonging. This emotion or feeling belongs to the cooperative system and is usually very powerful in various environments, including the domestic one, and can be a cause of suffering, if not a real pathology, when it entails self-sacrifice. Other emotions that belong to this system are *empathy*, *reciprocation* and *guilt*. The latter is present when we perceive to have failed to fulfill a request of solidarity or to have betrayed a loyalty pact.

The activation of this system, present only in man and partially in anthropomorphic apes, deactivates temporarily the competitive system and entails the beginning of interactions between individuals who in that context perceive themselves as peers and are joined by a project or a common intent.

As we can see, many emotions, such as anger, anxiety, guilt and happiness can be attributed to different motivational systems; so it's extremely important that the individuals are able to relate synchronizing and staying in step with each other on the same system. When this doesn't happen, the emotions of each of the two related persons are "read" and interpreted by the other according to his motivational system that is active at that moment. An example can better explain what we have just said. If in a married or engaged couple one of the two is certain, for some reason, that the other wants to leave him/her, the attachment system will activate and he/she will feel an intense anger of separation. However, the other could interpret the partner's anger as competitive anger, or rather, as his/her attempt to prevail and to gain a position of power, and therefore, this brings the other to respond with even more intense anger by beginning an agonizing escalation of accusations. A hug and a reassuring attitude could instead put an immediate end to the conflict. As sometimes happens also between a mother and her child, these lack of synchrony ("to dance together the same rhythm) and harmony ("to feel together the same way) can provoke discomfort and suffering in the related dyads. A lack of motivational harmony that often causes conflicts in couples, immediately arousing disappointment and anger for the certainty of "not being understood", is when one of the two seeks the contact of the other to obtain caregiving and comfort, or complicity regarding a specific project or goal, while the partner may feel excited and interpret the gesture as an implicit sexual request.

Lastly, following is a reflection on the way in which the emotions are perceived according to common sense. It's natural to think that to an external stimulus, such as walking in the countryside and suddenly finding ourselves before a viper, an immediate emotions of fear and alarm follows, that produces in turn an activation of the autonomic nervous system followed by the behavioral answer, usually escape. Although still controversial, different researchers proved that the physiological answer follows immediately the stimulus and only after several milliseconds we become aware of the associated emotion. (Theory of James - Lange) William James affirmed: *"We are sad because we cry, angry because we strike, afraid because we tremble, and not the contrary...".* This means that the body answers automatically to the internal or external stimuli, preparing for the fight, the escape or the pleasure and we perceive these alterations that occur in our body as emotions.

We have mentioned how the way we feel emotions and especially the ability to manage and control them is different from individual to individual, in consequence of our innate predispositions, of the type of developed attachment and of our personal family history. In particular, it has been largely demonstrated how traumatic experiences, especially if protracted for a long time, experienced during childhood and adolescence in the domestic environment, can cause neurological alterations in the "emotional brain" and predispose to more or less serious psychopathologies, ascribable to the category of personality disorders and complex post-traumatic stress disorders. To retrace our history and to recognize the external causes of our sufferings through a valid psychotherapy along with, when necessary, by specific drugs, will be useful to free ourselves from pathogenic believes, self-destructive to ourselves and to others, and to have the ability to control our emotions and behaviors, and ultimately to control our life.

Development

Birth, mating and death are the three basic facts in the *life cycle* of an individual and are associated with kinship and lineage. Birth produces progeny and defines the primary bond mother-child that is the basis of all family and social structures. Mating builds bonds between two individuals and is the ground for marriage and kinship systems. Death leaves an empty place, waiting to be filled, in the family system. In all cultures these events have always been accompanied with ceremonies, called by the anthropologists "rites of passage", because they mark the passage of existence from one state to another. These are, the imposition of the name at birth, the rituals related to puberty that in the "primitive" human groups sanctioned the passage from childhood to adulthood, marriage, and finally funeral of the deceased. Other socio-anthropological moments such as the adolescence, disengagement from the original family and retirement have been added as crucial ones of the life cycle. To these normative events, we must add those called para-normative, namely those that don't fall within the normal development of the life cycle; hence sudden events as a child's death, an accident, the premature loss of a spouse, and so on.

The wanting to make them comprehensible and to ritualize these critical evolutionary moments, in order to give them a collectively shared meaning, arises from the need of containing and elaborating the powerful emotions that they raise within the persons in-

114

volved. Rituals have this function, as in the case of the death of a loved one, the professional weepers in ancient Greece and Rome, just as until a recent time the "chiangimorti" in Salento, were called by the community to cry and despair for the deceased with great emotional expressiveness along with his relatives to produce a kind of liberating catharsis. To further reiterate the necessity for survivors to reaffirm the triumph of life over death, the funeral is still often concluded by a ritual meal in which the abundance of food and drinks has a restoring and comforting function and the cheerfulness that slowly replace the mourning accompanies the deceased in his death journey.

Until a few decades ago, in southern Italy, the tragedy caused by the death of a child was somehow made more manageable and endurable through the ritual of throwing candies and comfits along the route of the funeral procession to attract other children of the town or of the neighborhood, in order to allow them to accompany the small coffin into the cemetery and to mitigate with their joyful cries the anguish of the relatives. Eduardo de Filippo has shown with great sensitivity and poetry this event in his film "Oro di Napoli".

Among the world populations similar ways to perform these rituals, are extended to the events of births, entry in adulthood and marriages. To execute its function, the ritual must be first shared with the community, whether it is made up of relatives and friends or extended to social groups, up to the evolvement of the whole nation. This ritual must also act with symbolic effectiveness, through strictly defined and repeatable gestures and procedures, on the conscious and unconscious imagination of the participants, in order to contain and elaborate the feelings and the powerful emotions aroused by the ritualized event.

Until a few years ago, childhood and adolescence were denominated developmental age, considering reaching adulthood between 16 and 21 years, as a finish line that a human being is now mature and no longer susceptible to development. This concept of life cycle has been now abandoned and nowadays the approach of considering human being, from birth to death, in constant evolution and transformation prevails. If it's true that our body development, depending on different growth factors and hormones, is very fast and evident from birth to 15-20 years of age and sometimes even further, all somatic cells continuously die and renew themselves during the entire duration of our life. Also the development of the brain that was believed to end after 20 years of age, followed by a slow and constant neuronal degeneration, actually continues to develop, although slowly, until biological death.

The Italian scientist Rita Levi Montalcini was awarded the Nobel Prize in Medicine in 1986 for her discovery of nerve growth factor (NGF) that is present in cerebral cells and allows the regeneration and the restoration of the damaged neuronal networks as well as the growth of new structures during the whole life of the individual.

In psychology it is customary to define and study separately the three spheres of the development that are the sentimental, cognitive and social ones. The child's first experiences in the primary relationship with his mother leads to the formation of the Internal Working Models, namely to the formation of the internal representations of himself and of the surrounding world. These work as a filter, between the individual and the real world, that pre-selects the information coming from the environment before sending them to the brain's perception and processing centers.

In the case of secure attachment, the acquired confidence in ourselves and in others, will allow an harmonious development of thought processes, of social skills and of the ability to build resistant and satisfying emotional bonds. In the last few years the concept of *resilience* has been introduced; a term borrowed by the engineering vocabulary and that indicates the ability of a material to withstand the mechanical and thermal stress. In the same way, this term is used to indicate the ability of an individual to overcome the stressful effects of a trauma, avoiding the onset of a PTSD, a post-traumatic stress disorder that usually produces extremely distressing and disabling symptoms even after a long period.

A child with a secure attachment will have greater possibilities of mastering the traumatic events to which he may find himself exposed to, namely he will have a high resilience. To give an immediately comprehensible example: in a sexual harassment, mistreatments or abuse attempts by an adult or older mates, suffered by a child even of young age, he will

be able to perceive the incongruity and the danger-
ousness of the situation and will immediately contact
his parents for help without the fear of not being listened and understood or worse, of being accused of
lying. Furthermore, he will never repress his emotions or doubt his sensations. The trust in caregivers
will lead this child, if he needs it, to ask for help and
to expect help and also to provide help when required
in all his affectional bonds that he will build during his
life, beginning from his elementary school teacher to
his intimate friend. His experience will led him to con-
struct inside the certainty to be unconditionally loved,
not only if he demonstrates to be good, kind and obe-
dient, but also because he knows to be worthy and
deserving of love. The deep internalized conviction of
being unconditionally lovable (unconditional love) is
what characterizes the secure attachment (type B)
this increases in turn the resilience and strengthens
self-esteem. Self-esteem will allow to always have
the most possible choices in life, from choosing a
partner to the type of job performed, and will allow to
better manage the conflicts arising from competitive
situations.

The child that will have instead developed an insecure attachment (type A, C or D), will face greater
difficulties during his development and in general during the whole course of life. I want to remember that
the insecure attachment means to be insecure every
time such a system is activated, that is when the individual experiences anxiety and fear in respect to situations perceived as dangerous for his survival, and in
most cases, not as a permanent state of insecurity. A

child or an adult with avoidant attachment A, for example, could appear self-sufficient and very self-confident and show excellent performances at school or at work, maybe even to be recognized as a leader in certain contexts, but he could instead face with much difficulty the experiences of abandonment and mourning and carefully avoid long lasting emotional bonds to defend himself from such experiences.

The experiences of loss, mourning and abandonment activate the expectations of caregiving with the methods learned in early childhood. With regard to social life and emotional bonds, the Internal Working Models correlated with the insecure attachment lead to systematically implement strategies of defense against the eventuality of destabilizing and therefore extremely feared situations. The psychic energy employed to satisfy the needs related to safety will be subtracted from the needs of satisfaction, from the exploration and search for new experiences and opportunities. Without affirming to discover universal laws, we can therefore say that an insecure attachment protects less effectively from life traumas, complicates the construction of valid and stable bonds and in general, forces to develop low-key expectations or to compensate use of ineffective defenses as the idealization of oneself or the other, the rationalization or the denial of the need. The idealization allows to recover in some degree self-esteem for instance: I can convince myself to be different because I am superior to others because more intelligent, and by this I justify the fact of not being understood and my difficulties in socializing; or I can attribute this intellectual supe-

119

riority to the other in order to feel particularly lucky to know such an important person and to have his attention. Rationalization and denial allow instead to avoid the perception for the need of protection and love, by developing rational explanations and trivializing or denying outright the need itself.

Adolescence.

As the riddle of the Sphinx reminds us, the three ages of man are childhood, adulthood and old age. Adolescence is the fourth "age" brought on and defined mainly in western culture and accepted by everyone over the last century. The turning point which separates childhood into entry to adulthood is in fact given by the biological change that leads to puberty through maturation of the genitals with a strong intense desire to mate and in preparation to procreate, thanks to the release of large quantities of specific hormones in the body. After puberty, that can occur on average between the ages of 10 and 14, the body will continue to develop until it assumes its full adult form at around 16-20 year of age; but the biological age of adulthood is determined once the individual is ready to procreate. The definition of the intermediate phase between puberty and maturity, called adolescence, is a relatively recent cultural denomination in our history defined usually during the period of attendance in middle and high school and characterized by specific attitudes, conceptions and behaviors. Until the end of the nineteenth century, in fact, young adolescents within farming families worked the land or others were employed in factories along with adults to work more than twelve hours per day and were given meager salaries that did not even allowed them to appease their hunger. Unfortunately, in many Third-World countries, still nowadays, millions of children are forced to work for a few dollars per month or to fight in the numerous active conflicts in their countries, continuing to be deprived not only of their adolescence but also of their childhood.

In the majority of primitive societies, children grew up entrusted to women and were assimilated with them. Upon reaching puberty, the change of status from child to adult, was collectively sanctioned by rituals in which at the end, a new name was assigned, thus replacing the childhood one, and it was at that point that they were finally considered adults in every respect. Nowadays, we tend to identify adolescence with the time required by the young person to acquire an education, and up until the time he receives his certificate or degree, he is generally considered immature. In the past this was not true and immaturity was not attributed to the few young persons that, by virtue of their lineage, could attend regular teachings as the medieval "seven liberal arts" or, at a later time, the classes imparted in the first European universities. In fact, they had nothing in common with today's teenagers and didn't distinguished themselves for behaviors and attitudes but were equal to the adults, of the same wealth or same titles of nobility. The so-called "clerici vagantes", or goliards, as the students that attended the European universities were called, were young adults in every respect. As students of the universities that were the exclusive property of the Church, they had the same ecclesiastical privileges, even without belonging to the clergy. They were not subject to any judgment by the ordinary courts for possible crimes committed. Their feats such as those told, for example, in the manuscript Carmina

Burana, known for the anonymous symphonic composition by Carl Orff, did not differed from those of other "cronies" of all ages, whether they were soldiers of fortune, friars or local lords, and showed no characteristic attributable to current adolescents.

Becoming adults hardly ever corresponded with the reaching of a determined biological age, the so-called mature age, but it occurred through a specific ritualized attribution, determined and defined by society.

In past time, within farming and artisan families, young girls could be given in marriage soon after the menarche (in ancient Rome they could be given in marriage at 12 years old) and in any case, young girls and boys, as soon as they were able, had to farm the land along with their parents or had to learn a trade by working very hard.

Within noble families, young men, when not initiated to an ecclesiastical career, were instructed at very early age to use weapons and it wasn't uncommon in the Middle Age or in the Renaissance to become captains or commanders of armed groups at only the age of 14 or 15. Conradin of Swabia was only 15 when he came to Italy by crossing the Alps with his army to reconquer the Kingdom of the two Sicilies (1268), while in the eighteenth century, Louis XV of France was crowned king at the age of 12 and was married at 15. Catherine de' Medici, in the sixteenth century, was imprisoned by the Florentines at the age of eight and became a queen by marrying King Henry II of France at only 14, Lucrezia Borgia was given in marriage by her father, Pope Alexander VI, to Giovanni Sforza practically at the same age.

In general therefore, the passage from childhood to adulthood was sanctioned at a physiological level by the somatic changes deriving from puberty, while at a cultural level the recognition of the social group sanctioned the change of status. Since the most obvious sign of this change, is given by the maturation of the sexual and reproductive ability, the rituals of passage included ceremonies that implied social control and rules over the sexual impulse, which was considered a powerful element, subversive for the established order. Such rules are, for example, circumcision in males and infibulation or clitoridectomy in females. Genital mutilations documented by ethnologists still represent a wide range of different types of mutilations. Luckily, today mutilations of young girls are more rare and sentenced by most of the world, while, it is not clear for what bizarre reason, the excision of the prepuce in boys is still regularly allowed and carried out in many "civilized" countries, justified by religious or by debatable hygienic reasons, even if practiced in aseptic environments and supposedly with less painful procedures.

Furthermore, the rituals of passage to adulthood, especially for males, was often characterized by having to overcome a test of courage and valor, which was often very painful and dangerous, in order to be finally admitted into the world of men and warriors. Many movies and documentaries have efficiently shown how cruel and sometimes lethal these trials could be.

Summing up, young boys and girls upon reaching puberty were considered adults and were called to carry out tasks and to take on adult responsibilities such as to look after younger brothers and sisters, work, fight or were sent to seminaries to become priests.

Adolescence, interpreted as a phase of unproductive life and dedicated exclusively to studying and "leisure" time, while waiting to grow up is a cultural result of modern western society, widely widespread through globalization. It is also characterized by emotional turmoil and mood instability due not only to the increase growth of hormones in the body but also to the fact of having to face the first emotional, sexual and competitive experiences with peers.

School education, nowadays compulsory and available to all, has led to the establishment of a transitional period lasting several years in which the young person, no longer a child but still not considered mature enough to be accepted in the world of adults, remains dependent upon his or her family for a considerably long period of time. Todays teenagers diligently adapt to a whole range of attitudes, behaviors and emotional state including rebellious young antagonists to the cultural representations defined and induced through the mass media, and social networks, (Facebook, Instagram, social chat lines, etc.)

As we have already said, the most important and significant event experienced by a child and his family remains the physical change that is caused by action of female and male sexual hormones which in a very short time leads to the development of genitals and to changes in the body. At this point, they need to quickly integrate and assimilate these somatic changes and need to elaborate new strategies of relationship with the external world. Moreover, the insecurities and the crises that many of them experience with regards to their physical aspect or to the fact of having or not certain qualities and capabilities in order to face school requirements, as well as the fact of having to compete with their peers in order to win over a boyfriend/girlfriend and to gain acceptance in the group, are all extremely correlated with the type of attachment developed during childhood and with the expectations of their family and of society. It is the pressure of parental expectations, based on the achievement of specific high objectives, that can give place to feelings of defeat and humiliation when they are not able to succeed in full to satisfy them, leading these young people to develop depressive syndromes or in some serious cases, suicidal pathologies.

Lastly, the *decisive* moment of this phase in the life cycle is constituted by *disengagement* from the family of origin, meaning the passage from the condition of childhood and adolescence dependency to the state of personal independence typical of adulthood. Sometimes, this passage, that is part of the normal process of identification proves to be very difficult and problematic, if not even impossible, because of serious family dysfunctions or pathologies. This topic will be reassumed in a later chapter. By *disengaging we mean* the achievement of a state of emotional independence and not necessarily just economic. We can for contingent needs continue to live as an adult in our parents' home but in any case keep full control of our own life.

Sex.

Until the fifties, at least in the western world, there was total ignorance in regards to sex since the subject was burdened by numerous taboos derived mainly from moral and religious constraints. Even mating, admitted with marriage, had to be aimed solely at the procreation of children and never aimed at the satisfaction of pleasure. Our grandmothers went to bed with a long and heavy nightgown, equipped with a specific hole around the genital area to allow the implementation of the nuptial duty, and often recited the formula: "I don't do it for my own pleasure but to give my children to God". But since sexuality is a powerful impulse, inevitably there where many ways to transgress the rigid moral laws. Sex was more accessible and socially tolerated for men but much less for women who, paid with devastating feelings of guilt, if not with their life, their escapades. Between 1948 and 1953, Dr. Alfred Kinsey published in two volumes the results of a research that was carried out with a team of doctors and psychologists, funded by the Rockefeller Foundation and obtained by interviewing a sample of thousands of males and females subjects. This research had the merit of planting the seeds for the sexual revolution that would take place years later. What emerged from this survey was the total ignorance that most people had, with regards to the role of sexual intercourse in the reproduction mechanism; and furthermore, that masturbation was highly practiced in secret by both sexes, even though it always accompanied with huge internal conflicts, with feelings of guilt, and it was also believed to be the carrier of all kinds of degenerative diseases, from tuberculosis to dementia. Such beliefs were authoritatively corroborated by many doctors. A revolutionary aspect of this report was the highlight placed on female orgasm and the actual pleasure experienced by women during intercourse, topics hitherto taboos and never thoroughly investigated by medical science. Kinsey also explored the phenomenons of homosexuality, extramarital sex and childhood sexuality. He can be considered as a pioneer of the so-called gender theory which proves how the sexual orientation of an individual is not strictly determined by chromosome 46, but it develops and strengthens itself in the cultural and domestic context that the newborn is welcomed in, and that it can also change over time.

Kinsey didn't publish his third volume because he became the object of a veritable media lynching by the clergy and conservatives who accused him of being homosexual, a pedophile, and also a communist wanting to destroy the youth in his country. In spite of this, his methods of research were later acknowledged substantially correct and even now, in the state of Indiana, the Institute that bears his name is still operational.

While Dr. Kinsey for his research relied only on interviews and questionnaires, a few years later, William Masters and Virginia Johnson undertook a survey on the physiological correlatives of sexual arousal and of orgasm in males and females, by using specific instruments, some already available such as polygraphs and video cameras, but also by developing innovative devices such as a transparent plexiglass penis with an integrated camera to detect vaginal contractions and blood supply during coitus and orgasm. In this way, data related to sexuality was no longer collected only from the accounts of the interviewed individuals, but were revealed directly "in loco". In their book "Human Sexual Response", published in 1966, the four phases that compose intercourse are explained: arousal, orgasm, plateau, which is the period of fulfillment, and resolution. Furthermore, it is revealed with incontrovertible data that a woman experiences an orgasm of an equal if not superior intensity than man, and that the greater pleasure derives from the rubbing of the clitoris and not from the vaginal walls, as instead was affirmed by Freud referring to the *genital* phase of his sexual theory. Kinsey, Masters and Johnson, with their works, broke the wall of hypocrisy and ignorance that surrounded sex in our society and gave an impulse to the sexual liberation, especially for future women. With the development of the birth control pill, women finally had the freedom to use their bodies to draw all the pleasure they desired through sex and to finally allow them to decide on the subject of maternity.

Sexual pleasure is potentially present, although in immature and incomplete forms, ever since childhood, since the receptors designated for such purpose dwell in the genital area. But it is only at the age of puberty that we witness a real hormonal explosion of excitement and desire. So, the development of the reproductive organs highlights the topic of satisfaction of

130

the sexual needs and this, once again, implicates the weight that society, family and individuals attribute to it.

Within the first three years of life, a child fully develops his or her *gender identity,* namely he or she perceive with certainty himself or herself as a male or female individual. A very common but rather simplistic conviction leads to believe that at the moment of conception two distinct and perfectly separated paths open: the one that leads to the masculinity with chromosomes XY and the other that leads to the femininity with chromosomes XX. However, the reality is that we become males or females in successive phases, and often not definitively, as the frequent cases of sex change even in adulthood demonstrate. Furthermore, in situations as hermaphroditism, transsexualism and homosexuality it is even more complicated to identify with certainty to which sex they belong to. The interaction between genetic heredity and environment is at its maximum for the individuation of the gender identity.

The hermaphrodites are individuals in whom during the prenatal phase, for genetic and/or hormonal causes, the sexual organs didn't completely differentiate and develop, consequently at birth they show external genitals not distinguishable with certainty as male or female. In the past there have been cases of genetically male children who were believed to be females, and were brought up in the as such; they finally assumed the female identity to the point of having to be operated at puberty to continue to feel as complete women. In other cases, children born in

131

hospitals and therefore immediately diagnosed as hermaphrodites by doctors, had their genitals surgically operated on soon after their birth to allow them to be coherent with their genetic makeup or/and with their parents' expectations.

Homosexuality and transsexualism are considered sexual deviances of a psychological origin, as they arise at a psychic and behavioral level and supposedly is originated after birth. Also a possible genetically determined predisposition has been hypothesized but the influence of social, domestic environments and often of traumas as violences and sexual abuses during childhood from adults of the same sex, remains to be determinant.

During the nine months of gestation the prenatal sexual development is completely determined by chromosomes and hormonal factors; if all goes well, from the second month onwards the sexual organs in the fetus will begin to differentiate and will progressively lead to the development of the uterus, ovaries and vagina in females and of the penis, prostate and testicles in males, that is of the internal and external genitals as they will appear at birth. But from this moment onwards the context will prevail placing its heavy mortgage on the determination of the gender identity.

The birth of a *son* or of a *daughter*, greeted immediately by the exclamation "It's a boy!" or "It's a girl!", puts a social label on the newborn and generates completely different and culturally determined behaviors in parents and in all participants to the event. Successively, the imposition of the name, the clothes, the behaviors of the parents, the toys and everything else will determine whether the child *will feel as a* male or female, *independently of the biological sex*. Just like in the language development that proceeds with the child's predisposition to verbal communication but develops in a specific language (English, Italian, French, Arabic, etc) is determined within a period of time under the influence of the language spoken by parents and other persons with whom he comes in contact with, in this same manner, the identification of male or female, even in the presence of an innate predisposition, occurs within the first years of life by means of the environmental influence.

This identity then assumes a specific role, built and moulded by the behaviors and the attributions, with respect to male and female, in the family where the newborn grows up and of the culture of the country in which he or she lives; in brief, he or she will learn not only to be a male or a female but also how to be one and what it entails in the context in which he or she will grow up. Being born in a European, North African or Asian country already poses many differences, just as in a Catholic, Protestant or Islamic one. In particular the female condition, which is often still subordinate in traditional patriarchal societies, will be affected by these differences, just as that of homosexuals and transsexuals ones. In addition, within a determined society, we can grow up in a more or less permissive or repressive family with respect to sex. Further, what also contributes to build the *role identity* are things like attending a public school or a private one managed by religious orders/persons, grow up spending time with boy scouts or spend time in the street with other children and so on.

Moreover, within this argument, we need to insert the subject of childhood sexuality, the "sexual" experiences that a child has had before puberty. I don't intend to speak here about the abuses perpetrated by adults on children, which pertains to perversion or psychic pathology, but about the sexual experiences between peers that in many populations are not only permitted and tolerated but even favored because they are considered preparatory for adult sexuality. All this allows us to clearly understand how genetic determine sexual identity, that is, the pair of chromosomes XX or XY, can only point the way of a predictable development of the individual with the release of male or female hormones in due time and stimulate the desire towards a potential partner. What will be my sexual orientation, what will I feel, think and with what methods will I act to find satisfaction and pleasure will be mostly determined by the social and cultural context and mainly by my life story.

Lastly, to feel arousal for a person of the same sex or of the opposite sex, contrary to what we may think, is never the outcome of a personal choice but the result of many innate and environmental factors that still have not been clearly identified or rather, they have not been *all* identified. Certainly, the premature experiences of situations that involve sexual pleasure produce a sort of imprinting that, consciously or not, will orientate our preferences and

134

choices. If a parent systematically contaminates the normal gestures of affection and protection or the playful interactions addressed to the child with more or less explicit maneuvers that lead him or her to feel sexual arousal or to carry out a real seduction, the child may confuse the friendship and emotional patterns in every social relationship with which he or she will in the future confront himself, with those pertaining to sexuality. Every teacher has had the experience of children, even very young, who in the classroom engaged along with their school mates, explicit sexual behaviors, for example by simulating intercourse, and by using an incongruous language for their age. These cases must always be reported because they could indicate a child's exposure to sexual abuse. Conversely, if a parent rejects with behaviors of explicit disapprobation or with disgust the first innocent explorations of sexuality acted out by the child, then he will probably learn to associate a sense of guilt to physical pleasure, perceived as dirty and wrong.

Lastly, in the case of paraphilias, as pedafolia, necrophilia, fetish, sexual orientation can lead to seriously pathological outcomes. In these cases so deviant from the norm, it may be possible to trace in the childhood's history a highly traumatic event that has "fixed" their sexual desire on specific situations or eroticized "objects".

The formation of the couple.

We have previously seen that the laws of evolution bring us to stay alive as long as possible and to pro-create numerous offsprings, that will live as long as possible to assure the survival of our genes and our species. We have to agree that Nature has done its job well: upon reaching sexual maturity, males and females of every species seem to fall prey of a frenzy that pushes them to look for one or more partners to mate. In general, we can say that the act of copulation seems always to be very urgent and desirable, given the frequency and obstinacy with which it is searched for and the time it occupies in the course of our whole life.

In the past, the presence or absence of sexual pleasure in females in oestrus of some mammals has been much debated, given that when we observe them mating, it seems to us, more an assault with rape than a shared act; however, the presence of the *ritual* that is expressed from the beginning with the phase of the *courting* doesn't escape the ethologists. The ritual provides the right connotation and the right meaning for what we believe to be the competitive behaviors of the sexual act.

Our human sexual behaviors, when they aren't conditioned by repressions and inhibitions, are amazingly similar to those of our close cousins Bonobo chimpanzees. Their females are always sexually willing and active as males. Furthermore, it is evident that both enjoy much this activity and are not subject

136

to restrictions and moral taboos, they use sex in every occasion and with every willing partner, also as a
ritual of pacification to put an end to quarrels. We
can affirm, quoting Freud, that the Bonobos are sexually polymorphous since they practice oral, anal and
genital sex, as well as manipulations of various kind
with individuals of both sexes.

Some researchers attribute to the lack of oestrus
and to the continuous sexual availability, that characterizes not only the Bonobos but also human females,
that in order to keep to themselves their offsprings'
father, they will provide sexual gratification that he
would otherwise seek elsewhere, thus abandoning the
mother and her cubs to their fate.

This hypothesis is based on some biological constants that characterize all mammals; first of all the
fact that the little ones are engendered, given birth
and breastfed by their mother. There are then two
other elements, variable from species to species, that
determine the manner with which the basic unity
mother - child is safeguarded and protected, and these are, the length of time that the child's dependence
on the mother and the quality of care the mother has
on the offsprings.

These elements will condition the males, length of
stay within the family nucleus and the type of in-
volvement they will have with females. Depending on
different cases, this may vary from few minutes required for mating to a much more prolonged stay over
time, up until reaching a permanent bond. In short,
the longer it takes to go from birth to adulthood and
the amount of care needed by the little one of the

species, more important will be the regular presence and the support role of the male. However this reasoning is partial, because it doesn't take into account that in many species of primates and other mammals the care of the little ones is entrusted only to the mother, as in felines, and she is helped, as needed, by the other females of the group, while the dominant males are on their own. Furthermore, among the gorillas, the dominant male mates with all the females, impeding the access to others, while the characteristic of sexual promiscuity of chimpanzees and Bonobos makes the recognition of fatherhood difficult.

As Aristotle affirmed, we are social animals and so driven to build lasting and important bonds with our fellows. This is achieved through the recognition of the consanguinity and the affiliation, interpreted as the assimilation of a stranger into the family group or clan.

The anthropological concept of culture defines everything that is produced by the man organized in societies; so not only the inventions and the material discoveries as the fire, the wheel, the bow and arrows or the hardware of computers but also the creations of the mind as myths, religions, music, painting, mathematics and the rules that characterize kinship systems. To be organized into groups has been since the beginning of our history a guarantee of survival. The beautiful cave paintings of Neolithic, discovered in different places of the planet, efficiently illustrate collective hunting scenes of bison or deer that supplied precious proteins to our ancestors. The need to hunt, also big animals as mammoths to ensure sufficient quantities of food for everybody, and obviously the need to defend themselves more efficiently from predators and from abuse of power on the part of competitors, has consequently led to the creation of groups of organized individuals with specific tasks, well defined by gender and age. It's the evolutionary step that allows the passage from the pack to the first social cell, the extended family, and so to the clan and the tribe, up to more complex social structures.

The maintenance over time of this primitive human group required the establishment of lasting bonds among its members, that is an alliance based on concrete and tangible requirements. The exchange of gifts and women was - and in some countries still is - an instrument with which the men materially consolidated their alliances.

To give one's daughter or sister in marriage to another man who will in turn reciprocate with his daughters and sisters, was the means to build and strengthen alliances between families. To offer a head of cattle or the orchard's first fruits to a neighbor, will put him in the condition of having to reciprocate and will make him an ally. This still happens today among good neighbors. A numerous and cohesive group will be winning compared to one constituted by only a few individuals in the fight for survival. This reality also assigns a vital function to the taboo of incest: endogamy, prevents establishing of groups of allied and organized families, and is therefore, evolutionarily losing. An anthropologist who asked a "savage" why he didn't marry his sister instead of giving her in marriage to another man, heard the answer:

"Why should I give up a brother-in-law who would help me in the hunting and to defend myself from enemies? The choice between endogamy and exogamy became, within a few generations, the alternative between marrying outside or dying outside.

The custom of giving families the task of combining marriages, still present in many Islamic countries, in monarchies and until a few decades ago also in our culture, depicts exactly this type of function to build and strengthen alliances. As an alternative or integration to the exchange of women, in many communities it was required for the groom's family to pay the so-called *price of the bride*, consisting for example, in a certain number of farm animals, to be delivered to the woman's family or instead in performing chores to the wife's family rendered by the man for a specific time. Similarly, instead to the bride who was given in marriage to a man belonging to a prestigious family, a dowry in money or in any case of valuables could have been requested.

As we can see from what we have up to now said, the so-called marriage of love, based on sexual attraction, complicity and sharing, without any economic and material interest, summarized in the saying "love on a shoestring", is a very recent cultural conquest. The overwhelming initial passion supported by the hormonal storm lasts at most a few months and has little to do with the challenging tasks and the loads of responsibility such as giving birth and bring up children in the best possible way. Before Christianity made it a strict moral norm, the primarily procreative purpose of the marriage was already high-

140

lighted in ancient Rome. Augustus, in favor of numerous children born into families, during one of his orations declared: "If we could live without women we would rather avoid this hassle, but since nature has intended that we could not live in peace with them nor live without them, we must look for the breed's preservation   rather than to seek ephemeral pleasures."

In essence, even though we have sex and we fall in love for our unique pleasure and personal desire, we are actually pushed by an instinct of which we are totally unaware to engender healthy and beautiful children to ensure the perpetuation of our genes.

However, the subversive push of sexuality must be regulated and managed by the intervention of the society that imposes its rules and its systems of shared values to ensure its own preservation.   Therefore, every population has chosen its ways to marry and start a family: a man with more than one wife (polygyny), a woman with more than one husband (polyandry), the monogamous couple, the duty to marry the older brother's widow, and so on. Homosexual unions, that in some populations are considered unnatural or perverse and even prosecutable by death, were instead tolerated or socially recognized in many civilizations of the past such as the Greeks and the Romans and in most cultures not belonging to the three major monotheistic religions, who have always been extremely repressive towards a free and conscious sexuality.

 Anyway, the cultural constant that accompanies all marriage present in all populations are the rituals, from the very sumptuous ones with a great exhibition of wealth to the most modest observed by many social realities. But all rituals, without exception, emphasize on *sharing as* the primary characteristic of every union. Among the American natives Navaho, for example, the marriage ceremony consisted in eating together from the same bowl of corn, just as it occurred among the Pawnee, in which the bride placed before the husband a dish containing the food to be eaten together. We can also recall the Roman marriage ceremony *cum manu,* denominated *confarreatio*, in which the father of the bride passed the power he held over her into the husband's hands, to sanction this the bride and groom shared and ate together, in honor of Jupiter, spelt bread.

Other cultural variants concern the spouses' domicile which could be a house of their own, or live in mother's family house (matrilocality) or that of the father's family (patrilocality) or a collective building such as the large tribal houses that welcomed many families who belonged to the same clan, typical of the Indians of the Iroquois Nation in North America.

The manners in which the husband's presence, material and sentimental, is perceived at his bride's side can be very diversified, as it has been accurately described in anthropologists' reports and by ethnographers of the nineteenth century. A very curious case of wife - husband's relationship was for example the one observed in the Ashanti's population of Equatorial Guinea. This population had a matrilineal family organization for which the males, after marriage, continued to reside in the maternal family home, executing in any case their husband's rights and duties with specific visits to wives' house for the time needed to implement them (denominated *visiting husband*). So, the children grew up in the house belonging to the mothers, grandmothers and aunts, together with the men of the family who were the reference male figure that looked after them and for whom they had high regard and displayed obedience; they were the uncle or the maternal grandfather and not the biological father. This puts to peace the Oedipus complex so dear to Dr. Freud.

The unilineal descent system can recognize a paternal or maternal "bloodline". In the first case the recognized ancestors will be the father, the paternal grandfather, the great-grandfather and so on while the women not related by consanguinity are affiliated. Conversely, in the matrilineal descent the men are affiliated and the generations are perpetuated from mother to daughter. Our kinship system is complex because it recognizes both lines of descents, even if not always at a juridical level.

These anthropological notions just mentioned, are intended to avoid falling into the ethnocentric trap of thinking that our form of marriage is the only admissible one and of even considering it a natural law; the only natural laws are those that push us to sexually mate and to look after the children until they reach the independence. How, where, with whom and for how long, are the user manuals and prerogatives of the culture developed by the different populations.

143

Back to our culture, the formation of an enduring couple and the establishment of a new monogamous family, composed of a man and woman able to look after their children as best as possible, is seen as a critical event, a moment of passage that entails also the approach, the contact and sometimes the collision between the two families involved, bringing in the new family their systems, and values that characterized them. Furthermore, it is in this phase, if not endured previously, that we have to take on and overcome two potentially traumatic situations, first to let go of our children and secondly to face the empty nest syndrome. To successfully let go of a child from the family means to allow him to be able to build his own identity, to become a distinct individual, to be detached from the "undifferentiated family ego mass", as the psychotherapist Murray Bowen denominated the family identity. If he is able to put a well-defined and recognizable boundary between his own emotions, expectations and life projects from those of his parents, brothers or sisters, he avoids in this manner to bring in the newly established family a dysfunctional and sometimes destructive heritage.

Another factor, if present, that can sometimes make it impossible for the child to leave the original family is the type of proxy that one or both parents may have given, more or less implicitly, many years before to their child. This psychological concept of proxy is closely linked to the need of compensation that emerges when the family is affected by a traumatic event, devastating and hard to process. An emblematic case is the premature death of a child to

144

which the birth of a second child follows, to whom the proxy may be given to compensate the great loss suffered by the parents, maybe even by giving him the same name as that of the dead child. The delegation forces the contractors, in this case parents and children, to respect *at any cost* the secret undeclared pact of loyalty, stipulated between them. The *cost* for the child will be to renounce the fulfillment of a personal life project and of any emotional bond potentially able to put at risk this pact. So, the attribution to a child with the same name of the mother's brother who prematurely died in a tragic accident, or of the paternal grandparent who committed suicide, entails almost always the risk of a proxy. The establishment of these systems of family loyalty, derived from attributions of delegations by one or more members of the family system at the expense of another in order to compensate mournings and other unprocessed traumas, that occurred sometimes generations before, inevitably determines great sufferings and internal conflicts exactly at the time of disengagement. This will be in fact perceived by the delegating parent as a real betrayal of the implicit stipulated pact.

The empty nest syndrome concerns instead parents who, at the moment of disengagement from the home by their children, who have become autonomous, have to deal with the powerful emotions that accompany the experiences of abandonment related to separations and the inexorability awareness of time passing. The parents who in turn didn't resolve their personal problems at the time when they left their home, will have many difficulties in tolerating and managing these emotions and can carry out, more or less consciously, different strategies to control them. The resistance of some parents to tolerate a longer physical and emotional distance from their children by now adults, has also given rise not only to an ironic and funny anecdote about the clashes between the parents-in-law and their respective sons-in-law and daughters-in-law, seen as those who stole their beloved son or daughter, but also to peculiar habits as observed in the past in some African populations in which ritualized behaviors of concrete physical avoidance of the mother-in-law by the groom were prescribed or there would have been terrible consequences. Evidently, it's the same all over the world and in any case the empty nest syndrome is easily manageable and surmountable and never evolves, contrary to the impossible disengagement, in real psychopathologies.

As we have just seen, the passage from childhood to adulthood can entails serious problems in the case of families characterized by dysfunctional dynamics. Moreover, the distress of separation and the fear of loneliness will reactivate the Internal Working Models correlated with the attachment system developed by the involved family members that, especially if it is of insecure type, will complicate further and enter into synergy with the above-mentioned dynamics.

Let's now limit ourselves to consider what currently happens in our society when two individuals are attracted to each other and decide to join together to form a couple.

The contracts of the couple

In the United States it has become common, since a few years, to stipulate a written contract between the two persons who join in marriage. In this contract the rights and duties of both spouses are indicated in detail, purposely in case of a subsequent possible divorce. This procedure has been consolidated especially among personalities such as actors, athletes and descendants of very wealthy families. Although this is, at least at the present time, only an extreme case, it is useful to mention it for our purposes because it highlights and assigns an institutional value to the series of reciprocal expectations that each of the two spouses have on the other. The most common examples that could fall in this "contract" concerns the division of the housework, the will to preserve their hobbies and personal interests after marriage, the economic domestic management, the manners of having sex, procreation and raising of children, social roles, the displays of affection in public and in private, and so on. A kind of " instructions for the marriage" that the two spouses have agreed to put in place and to share. They define how the four wheels on which the couple's car lies and proceeds, should turn: affectivity, sexuality, sociability and intellectual curiosity. We will call this first contract explicit because it is clearly present on the level of the consciousness and can be verbalized, shared and renegotiated at any time by both spouses. The non respect of the terms of the contract can cause conflicts and a certain degree of suffering in the couple.

But the couple stipulates too - we could say without their knowledge - a second and more important contract, not declared and partially unconscious, that gathers the expectations concerning the affective and emotional sphere, the cure and the compensation of the unresolved traumas of our childhood and adolescence, the certainty of having met him or her who will do finally justice to whatever we have experienced as a deprivation in the past. We will call this contract implicit because it can't be explicitly claimed, it can't be gasped or recognized by the partner and above all, since it is not formulated, it can only be supposed that it is shared. It's evident that there will be two versions of this contract, each one in possession of each of the spouses and considered legitimate because each of the two supposes that the other, driven by genuine love, has *implicitly* understood and accepted it.

Obviously the "weight" of this kind of secret pact will be very different depending on the type of attachment and on the personal life history that characterizes each of the spouses.

To give some examples, we can list a series of these possible implicit expectations among the most common ones, trying to translate them into spoken language.

I will save you. You will have to protect me because I'm weak. At least you won't leave me. You have to guess my needs and desires even if I don't show them. You will never betray me. You mustn't

149

disappoint me. You will be the perfect mother/father that I hadn't. And so on.

As you may have noticed, they are rather different statements from those normally uttered by the priest/minister or the judge during the wedding ceremony. These expectations concern in fact the deep needs of security; they are related to the kind of attachment developed during childhood and to the traumatic events present in the family and personal history of each one. So, the couple bond proposes again, if there haven't been changes in the meantime, those secure or insecure, avoidant ambivalent or disorganized models, developed during the first years of life. A man who as a child didn't feel loved and was cared by his mother, by obtaining her attention only when "he was a good boy", will tend to seek confirmations and reassurances in the couple, continuing to be good and complaisant, but with the firm belief of being in any case inept and of not being able or worthy to be loved. A woman, abused or sexually molested in the family during childhood, may have developed the belief of having merit only as a sexual object and could project on the partner, with great suffering, this prejudice.

In as much as the implicit contract of the couple will be practicable for both parties, that is in the cases in which each one can answers rather efficiently to the other's expectations, the couple will prove to be sufficiently strong over time.

Furthermore, the problems that a couple could face, could also be resulting from a failed or imperfect disengagement of one or both from their original family. In fact, to join in a couple means to give birth to a new family, whether there will be children or not, and this means that the relationships with the family of origin have to be reviewed and renegotiated to avoid intrusions, interferences and confusions. Between the new and the old family there must be a boundary that delimits and defines the different areas of belonging and pertinence. The family psychotherapists often use the concept of co-evolution, valid for all individuals united in plots of family relationships, to reiterate the need of the parents to evolve together with their children, accepting the reality of the passage of time and positively embracing the changes in the roles that this entails. All of us are able to intuit how dysfunctional an interaction parent is, both adults, in which the first one insists on imposing his own vision of the world and his choices, continuing to perceive his son as a child still needy of protection and guide.

Another way of keeping a son tied to oneself, even more deleterious, is one resulting from roles reversal, this happens when the adult son or daughter are called to take care, in an improper and dysfunctional manner, of one or both parents who openly show their need to be looked after and not "abandoned". This family relational model begins far away in time, usually in early childhood, and in it the normal relationship of caregiving parent - child is completely reversed. A sad and seriously depressed mother will tend to seek comfort in her child, even if very young, telling him and sharing her discomforts and seeking his closeness only for her own solace, delegating the

151

unwitting but effective role of therapist to him. In these cases the new family composed of the young spouses will never find a place in the mind of this parental child while the other spouse, if he or she doesn't rebel, will be co-opted, absorbed, in the spouse's family that will emotionally experience, as well as de facto, as the only possible family.

It's useful to specify that these briefly mentioned dynamics concern the mental, emotional and affective sphere of the individuals and so they entail concepts as loyalty, care, belonging and aren't affected by material situations such as the greater physical closeness or distance. A young couple in financial difficulties can also live together for a period in the house of one's parents, but if the disengagement will have been effective, he will succeed in applying and maintaining the necessaries boundaries with the latter. In the same way, a young man who hasn't really disengaged from the family of origin, will continue to bring the family inside, internalized, even if he moves to the other side of the world.

We talked in broad terms about the problems that can arise in the couple, but not how they occur. A good metaphor to indicate how the two individuals of the couple bind together is to see them joined at the head, belly and genitals. The head represents the shared parts that concern the convictions, beliefs, intellectual interests; the belly symbolizes the emotional and affective sharing as the bond with their children; the genitals represent the sexual attraction and desire.

152

The impracticality of the secret pact or the inter-
ference of the families of origin, as we have just seen,
will create conflicts in the couple that will manifest
with dysfunctions in one or more of these areas. So,
we can close ourselves in, with the inability to give
words to our emotions and the firm conviction of being totally misunderstood by the spouse. Or we can
attack him/her through manipulative maneuvers on
the children and other members of the family, to dis-
credit our partner in their eyes or to find alliances
against him or her. Lastly, we can implement a sexual "protest" and the rejection of physical contact, justified or not by pathologies as the well-known "head-
ache". The latter is the favorite strategy, often partially unconscious, to strike the spouse without con-
fronting each other about the true reasons of the conflict, for which many sexual "problems" as the premature ejaculation, impotence, frigidity and the loss of
desire should be interpreted as an alarm, a red light,
that leads to more serious reasons and not to pathologies on their own.

The couple's dysfunctions that manifest with the
belly, that is those in which, more or less consciously,
the children are used to strike the spouse, risk causing a considerable suffering to them. A parent who
force a child to take sides against the other parent,
builds a pathogenic relational scheme called "perverse
triangle", especially when it is realized at the expense
of a very small child who is consequently unable to
understand, manage and communicate these domestic dynamics. A simple example will help us to better
understand the kind of psychological damage that this

153

manipulative strategy, carried out by one parent, can cause to a child. A woman who seems clearly unhappy, accusing her partner of being rough, ignorant and brutal could seduce her male child by educating him to become the opposite of his father, positively reinforcing his artistic sensitivity and devaluing any intention of practicing competitive activities, thus allowing him to side against the father. The risk that the man perceives the son as an enemy and attacks the child because he sees in him as an effeminate ally of the mother is very high. Similarly, a father could seduce a daughter making her feel the ideal woman he has always desired and never found, full of sweetness and femininity, devaluing the mother, described as an insensitive woman, frigid and unable to love. It is useless to reiterate how such situations can cause irreparable damages to the so perversely triangulated children.

To end this brief excursus on the couple, I consider it opportune to reiterate that there is no valid recipe to ensure a positive outcome of the conjugal couple. Advice often given by friends such as: to always tell the truth, or rather to always deny, or even to try to solve every conflict using mediations or compromises, turn out to be useless. Each couple is unique and not reproducible and the success of union between two individuals lies only in the ability to understand and make the implicit or secret pact viable, in addition to the declared one, for the benefit of both. Ultimately, also two individuals who tend to relate to each other with sado-masochistic manners and who with "normal" partners would face considerable difficulties, could give life to a very harmonious and functional couple, even if a little eccentric, if they succeed to make their secret pact viable. This can be seen in the film "Secretary", released a few years ago, were the two protagonists successfully managed to do just this. This film that won a special prize at the Sundance Film Festival in 2002, tells the story of a self-destructive and masochistic girl who, just dismissed from the psychiatric clinic, looks for and finds a job at a law firm, were the young lawyer, in turn, gradually reveals his sadistic and punitive tendencies. Their complementary ways to seek sexual pleasure, in him orientated to inflict pain and in her to obtain physical punishments, will gradually lead them to enjoy more and more their original intercourses to the point of getting married and living happily ever after.

So, the ways of being a couple are innumerable, as human history has amply demonstrated, and the pretension to impose a model based on determined ideological and religious values, reputed to be "natural", is one of the strategies that pertains to social control and not to anthropological psychology.

A child is born

All myths and religions developed by different peoples have tried to give a sense to the event of birth (Where were we before?) and of death (where will we be after?). Regarding birth, some native Australian ethnic groups believed that a woman could get pregnant passing by chance through a specific sacred place, such as a grove or a source, where the unborn children dwelled; her husband would have known of conception because he would have dreamed the child that night.

A myth collected by the ethnologists during the observation of a primitive human group, reported by the historian of religions Mircea Eliade, tells how death is necessary to allow our children to live. In mythical time, as in the Eden, there wasn't death and the individuals never get old, staying forever young. Just like snakes, at regular intervals, people too change their old skin to renew themselves. But one day a woman changed her skin soon after having given birth to her child; the latter, not recognizing her mother from her old smell of the skin soon after the transformation, began to cry desperately for fear and refused her breast. After many fruitless attempts the woman, seeing that her child was dying, decided to put back on her old skin. The child was saved but, from that moment on, the woman and all other human beings had to accept to die. So, in this case it isn't an act of disobedience punished by a choleric and vindictive God what condemns us to die, but the necessity of an act of love.

Coming back to the birth of a child, we have to remember how, in all human groups, he or she wasn't considered really "born" until the imposition of the name. Only after this ceremony, in fact, the newborn could be officially welcomed in the social group, while up to this time he/she remained in a state of suspension; also in the Catholic religion, where the ritual of the imposition of the name occurs in baptism, the non baptized children weren't considered members of the community so that, in the case of premature death, they were doomed to Limbo, a sort of nobody's land. Only in 2007 this "non-place" was declared nonexistent by Pope Benedict XVI.

The imposition of the name to the newborn creates and defines the different roles within the family system: two parents, four grandparents, maybe some of the eight great-grandparents, brothers, sisters, uncles, aunts and cousins, to limit ourselves only to our denominations of kinship relations.

These roles are culturally defined and determinate, meaning that to them is attributed a set of attitudes, behaviors, attributions and emotions that not always correspond necessarily with the biological bonds; this happens, for example, in the case of adoptions and affiliations. Every human group, whether it is primitive or civilized, defines and characterizes in a peculiar way the family system and the roles within it.

The anthropologist Robin Fox lists the four constants that are at the roots of all kinship systems of all cultures; the first two of them are indisputable because they belong to the already mentioned biological events, the other two are incontrovertible because have always been present in human history.

Principle 1. Women engenders and raise children. The dyad mother-child can be considered the primary cell, the basic unit from which every social and family structure originates.

Principle 2. Men fecundate women.

Principle 3. Men exercise control. In human history, even if there have been cultures where the decisions for the community and the ownership of the land were delegated to women, as in the Iroquois Nation of the Northwest American Indians, the wars of conquest for the control of the resources were always men's prerogative. There have never been female warriors: Amazons belong to myth and only recently women soldiers, in United Stated and Israel, have obtained the right to fight together with men, or rather as men, on the front line.

Principle 4. Incest is taboo. Only in some dynasties, such as those of the Pharaohs in Ancient Egypt, the consanguineous marriages were not only allowed but sometimes even imposed to preserve the purity of blood that was considered to be of divine origin and that, for this reason, couldn't be mixed with the blood of ordinary mortals. These same considerations based on blood have led in the past many royal families, in different countries, to practice endogamy, that is to get married in the family, thus perpetuating over time serious hereditary pathologies.

Considering these four principles as a universal basis, the human cultures that have been established and developed throughout history, have been able to develop, just like the different languages, a constellation of innumerable and different systems of kinship, marriage and social structures. Levi-Strauss, paraphrasing Freud, affirmed that a child at birth is "socially polymorphic", ready to join and integrate in the human group, whatever it is the one to which he/she will belong.

The imposition of our model of civilization, economically and technologically dominant, on the subordinate cultures has led by now to their almost total disappearance. A significant acceleration of the genocide practice, always present in man's history, occurred after 1492 with the extermination of tens of millions of American natives, with slavery practiced for centuries at the expense of Africans, with wars on colonial conquest and with forced evangelization of the "savages".

The book "American Holocaust" by David E. Stannard (1994) describes very exhaustively the history of mass destruction of the whole pre-Columbian societies and cultures, carried out with the pretension to impose "civilization" and the worship of the one true God on the natives, but actually motivated by an out of control avidity and racism.

From the discovery of fire and later of the techniques of domestication, animal husbandry and agriculture, man has begun to intervene on the laws of evolution with a more and more strong impact on the natural environment, provoking over time the extinc-

159

tion of thousand of species and the irreversible modification of every kind of planet habitat. The acquisition of the ability to impart by cultural way a more and more large quantity of information, integrated with genetic transmission, has led the human species to be able to manipulate the evolution at will, acting heavily on the environment that hosts it.

Just as it happened and is still happening to the biological diversity, were many species of plants and animals are by now extinct, also many cultural diversities have disappeared because they have been destroyed or made subordinate and assimilated to the winning model. A model characterized by the continuation of a technological development, always motivated by the need of control and dominion that doesn't produce a corresponding real human progress, and by the frenzied exploitation of the planet resources. As in a sort of inverted parabola, the laws of evolution that over millions of years have led slowly from the unity of the original primordial cell to the marvelous complexity and diversification of the living world, today they are allowing the progressive destruction of all this diversity through the work of man, with its technology he has acquired the necessary tools to bend the world to his needs. The evolutionary law that guaranteed the survival only to the individuals more adapted to the context, when it is eluded modifying and in some cases destroying this context, that is our habitat and that of many other living species, is likely to lead us to catastrophe. The technology that we have today and that we incessantly use to exploit the planet draining even its last resource, polluting the oceans and the air that we breathe, makes this emergency even more dramatic and makes the destiny of our world, considered as a living entity called Gaia by many scientists not salaried by the multinationals, sinisterly look like that of an organism devoured by the metastasis of a cancer.

Resuming the event of birth, we can now sum up what we have so far tried to tell. There are motivational pushes for survival, originated from the most ancient parts of the brain, that don't entail the need of interaction with another individual, such as the predatory system, the defense system and the exploratory system. Then, there are motivational interpersonal systems that instead entail always a bond with another significant individual such as attachment-caregiving, competition, sexuality and cooperation; and we have seen as the acquired manners of implementation of these motivations (Internal Working Models) can change. Lastly, there are the mental collective representations induced by the family and the community that give a meaning and emotionally qualify the different kinship roles and in particular the bond mother/child. Let's try now to understand what contributes to give shape to this specific bond and what differences can be detected by the multicultural observation.

In order to detect and study these differences, before the last world war in the United States, a movement of psychologists and anthropologists arose, called "Culture and Personality", that intended to analyze the constants and the variables observed in the child rearing systems in different cultures, taking as reference the Freudian theories. To have an idea of how they can change, it's sufficient to reflect, brushing up on our scholastic culture, on how different the bond between a Spartan mother and her son, who was taken away long before puberty to entrust him to gyms and to the education of weapons and war, was by comparison with the equivalent of Athens, city state and cradle of democracy, protector of the arts and home of great thinkers, or finally of Corinth, devoted to Aphrodite and unpopular with the Apostle Paul for its freedom of customs.

All of us, our behaviors, our way of thinking and feeling, our vision of the world, are the result of a very complex interaction between individual, sociocultural and environmental factors. To say that we are our past doesn't mean only to affirm that we are the product of our individual history but also that our identity is deeply rooted in Human History.

The previously used image of the "matryoshka" turns out to be therefore a precise metaphor: in the "form" shaped by the social group there's the form of the family that in turn contains the dyadic bond mother-child that in turn contains the individual.

So enunciated, it would seem, and maybe it is, a very deterministic description; but the neocortex, that luckily we have, makes us flexible and allows us to act on our destiny within certain limits.

Let's dwell now upon a little considered aspect; the fact that together with the child two parents, a mother and a father, characterized by specific roles, must be born. Factors such as the age, the social class, ideologies or the belonging to a specific religious

162

creed are, as we have seen, certainly determining to define these two roles, but the predominant element, often partially inaccessible to consciousness, is given by the family history. The psychoanalyst Selma Fraiberg writes: *"In every nursery there are ghosts. They are the visitors from the unremembered past of the parents; the uninvited guests at the christening. The intruders may break through the magic circle, and a parent and his child may find themselves reenacting a moment or a scene from another time with another set of characters"*. (1974)

It's the unremembered and undeveloped past relating to the history of at least three generations of ancestors that breaks in without declaring itself in the perceptions, emotions, beliefs, and behaviors of the new parents, and so the larger the number of the highly traumatic events in the family history is, especially if kept secret, the more difficult will be to keep out of the room these ghosts. Nowadays, cinema and literature have made the themes of the tendency to the repetition of the trauma and of the intergenerational transmission of child rearing models familiar also to the general public; we know that the man or the woman, mistreated and humiliated or sexually abused during childhood within their family, will have many probabilities, if not adequately cared-for, to repeat again this dysfunctional model of relationship towards their children.

A man who had suffered serious mistreatments and humiliations from his father during childhood, couldn't hold his devastating anger when he felt challenged by his son who was only six years old; even loving him

163

tenderly, in that case he literally lost control and un-leashed his anger with great emotion, scaring to death the child who in those moments really con-vinced himself that his father wanted to kill him. All the pain and the furious rage that this man had felt when he was a child against his father, by never ex-pressing them for fear of further punishments, irrupt-ed unconsciously and vehemently when he perceived a provocative or challenging behavior in his son. The victim of the past became the persecutor in the pre-sent. This mechanism had already been intuited by the psychoanalyst Sandor Ferenczi who had coined the definition "identification with aggressor" to place it within his theoretical construction.

So the birth of a child can determine a *bringing up to date* of the unremembered traumas suffered during childhood. The 2005 film "The Beast in the Heart" by Cristina Comencini, based on the novel written by herself, dramatically highlights this eventuality.

The theme of the passage from one generation to another of the effects of any family drama kept se-cret, or unsolved, appears always very important in all emotional bonds, not only in those between a par-ent and his child, because it will determine their quali-ty and functionality. An example will help us to better understand what we have said.

A young woman asked for psychotherapeutic help because, even if she was very successful in her work and social life, every time she tried to build a stable emotional bond she unintentionally started to sabo-tage it soon after, by letting a part of herself extreme-ly punitive, controlling and sadistic towards her man, unexpectedly emerge and. The narration of the family history, didn't seem to initially report particular traumatic events, but it showed a particular feature: a strong emotional and sympathetic bond along the maternal line, from generation to generation, that is between daughter, mother and grandmother up to the great-grandmother, and at the same time it showed a depreciation, often very close to contempt, also detected by the unusual poverty of information in the reconstruction of the genogram*, for all the men of the family.

These were described very negatively in the story and were often humiliated, despite missing concrete reasons to justify such attitude.

This woman couldn't give a really convincing explanation of the origin of these behaviors, if not the one derived from the prejudicial belief that men are fundamentally unreliable and traitors and consequently they must be kept in subordinate condition and carefully controlled. Every time that a love story started to strengthen itself, becoming a stable bond, the young woman started to suspect treacheries and even perversions in the partner, executing intrusive and obsessive behaviors such as controlling secretly his mobile phone, his e-mails and his personal effects, looking for any evidence of his presumed infidelity and unreliability.

*The genogram is a tool used in psychotherapy that allows the patient to reconstruct together with the therapist a narration of the history of his family using also a graphic visualization, old photos and films, when they are available, of all its members.

165

During therapy, invited to seek further information from some distant relatives on the evident's "black holes" present in her family history, the woman finally discovered the origin of this script, unconsciously inherited down the female line, that prevented her from building a good couple relationship. It was an event that happened more than a century before and that was kept strictly secret: her great-grandfather, married and with already grown children, had seduced and got pregnant a barely pubescent girl, causing a huge scandal in a small town in southern Italy where he lived. On the run and chased by his relatives, he committed suicide by hanging himself in a uninhabited farmhouse and leaving an ignominious stigma on his descendants.

At a distance of four generations, the anger and the shame aroused by this event, were still present in this unaware great-granddaughter. After many sessions devoted to the elaboration of this traumatic revelation, the woman began slowly to look at the real man that she had chosen and that she loved, freeing herself from the perverse and psychologically devastating ghost of her ancestor.

Another case concerned a young mother who, when her daughter turned six, had a sudden psycho-physical collapse associated with the re-emergence of memories, separated from her consciousness, that were related to the sexual abuses inflicted by her father, and which had started when she was exactly as old as her daughter.

These examples that we have reported are obviously extreme cases and normally the birth of a child does not re-emerge anything so traumatic, but it certainly puts into play, for all, the positive and negative experiences of our childhood, and this must be taken into account.

So, to become parents requires to take on a very challenging path of personal growth and at the same time to become aware of what being mother or father meant for the respective families of origin, in terms of roles and responsibilities, and to be able to manage possible traumatic events, not yet resolved or elaborated.

Adulthood

The phase of the life cycle that goes from the birth of one or more children, up to the time they become adults and in turn also parents, puts us before a game of mirrors in which, looking at us, we recognize our parents and, at least in part, all the other significant members of our family of origin. This can either be a pleasant feeling, or it can make us hate the similarities that we will inevitably discover, even if we believe that we have done everything to avoid their mistakes. As we have already mentioned several times, we couldn't prevent the past from bursting, in a more or less incisive manner, into our present, especially the unremembered past. Carl Gustav Jung wrote: *"Until you make the unconscious conscious, it will direct your life and you will call it fate."*

The way we will react to difficulties, but also to the opportunities, of life, independently from the path of personal growth, will in any case be affected to some extent by the models learned and elaborated from our own family history. How will we react to a school bullying episode that occurs to our child? Or to an offer of a permanent job abroad? What will it mean to be father and mother, wife and husband, brother and sister in our family? Will our children freely choose their way, whatever it is, or will we choose for them the course of their studies? They are apparently simple questions that, however, require complicated answers.

But in the course of adult life there can be events that require answers even more complicated and full of consequences, as a separation or a divorce, the impossibility to have children, a dismissal from work or the failure of our company, to mention a few. Last in order of time, but not in order of importance, for the purposes of preserving our self-esteem and the feeling of having control over our life, is the arrival of the last working day, retirement. Let's briefly examine some of these events that, if not mastered effectively, can be perceived as catastrophes that can destroy our existence.

"Till death do us part" is the formula with which the wedding ceremony ended. But the up to date statistics tell us that, in Northern Europe, almost one of every two marriages ends with a separation or a divorce before a judge. When it goes well we separate by mutual consent, finding an agreement on the division of assets and, in case of children, on their custody. Quite often the phrase "I declare void the marriage of..." sanctioned a state of permanent conflict between the ex spouses who will resort to any means, legal and not, to hurt each other. This happens when the pain of loss and the experience of abandonment are prevailed by rage, the destructive fury, that comes from humiliation and defeat and from the fear of losing, with the end of the marital relationship, also the relationship with our children. But we can't divorce from our children, on the contrary the parenting duties become even more specific and burdensome because defined and properly regularized by law. In any case, the rupture of the emotional bond of the

169

couple, activates strong emotions of fear and insecurity and requires activation all the personal resources to get by. Once again, these resources will be strongly related to the type of attachment and to the family and personal history of the individual.

To resort to a couple psychotherapy or to the intervention of a family counselor, we can avoid in many cases situations of permanent conflict or of competitive stalemate that, in addition to undermining the psychophysical equilibrium of the contenders, would cause serious problems to the children who, even if not explicitly, would be in any case called upon to take sides in favor of one or the other parent. We wrongly believe that it is better not to separate when there are young children, even if this means to make them grow up in a context characterized by continuous quarrels and tensions; actually, children need primarily the truth and not to be in situations of cognitive dissonance between what they perceive and what we tell them.

Instead a separation between spouses with teenage children could determine in the latter a slowdown or, worse, an interruption of their life cycle phase, the one that concerns the disengagement and the entrance into adulthood. The moving of the family "focus" on immediate problems of emotional and material reorganization, especially in case of open conflict of the parents, will place the child's equally urgent problems to the background and so they will feel deprived of the attention and the necessary support needed, and they could manifest their suffering and their an-

170

ger in many ways, even resorting to sociopathic behaviors.

Also the unfulfilled desire to have children can become for some individuals an element of self-depreciation and can introduce elements of instability of the emotional bond. We can resort to adoption or foster care of a child, but it may happen that, over time, that a set of problems can emerge in these cases related to prejudices and beliefs, deeply-rooted and defensively denied, on the effects of the unknown biological heritage that will weighs on the adopted child.

Let's face now the theme of the cessation of the working activity and of retirement, an event placed by the sociological research in the first places among the causes of stress together along with moving from one place to another and the death of a partner.

Some people accept with joy, or at least with serenity, the time of retirement, appreciating the opportunity to have all the time they want to devote themselves to the activities and interests for which they have always had a passion, and to which they couldn't dedicate themselves as they wanted up to this time. In this case it's clear that the self-image that these individuals had built during their life wasn't based exclusively on professional achievements or on the climb to higher positions in the corporate hierarchy, but also or mainly on other values as family relationships, culture, arts, sport and anything else that is susceptible to maintain and increase self-esteem. But in other cases, stopping a working activity is experienced as the activation of the reserve fuel indicator, the irrepa-

171

rable loss of the most important part of themselves, followed by an experienced mourning that, if not properly faced, can lead to a depressive syndrome with important somatic repercussions. In these cases, to recover interest in the lives of others, to participate in group activities, to explore the possibilities that life still offers, to take care of their health and body, can be an efficient remedy.

To be lucky enough to get to the so-called third age, puts the individual before the reality, hardly acceptable, of the transformation of his image similar but opposite to that experienced at the time of puberty. Also in this case there will be, evident somatic and hormonal changes that will affect sexuality and body appearance and that will force us to rethink and redefine our ways of relation with the others.

To move towards the so-called third age puts us also before the loss of loved ones and of important emotional bonds as that of our parents, colleagues, friends and partners. The death of a person to whom we were closely related with, such as a parent or a spouse, causes a fracture in the flow of life that defines a before and an after, and this before and this after will be very different because they will entail the necessity of placing us again in the system of our affective relationships, by adapting ourselves to an absolutely new situation. The most concrete evidence of this deeply changed reality, in the case of the loss of parents or elder brothers and sisters, is given by the awareness that, except for extraordinary events, the next time will be our turn. And this reality will be spread as an halo effect: it will touch our children, our grandchildren, and it will be shared with our friends.

There are many studies on the phases of the mourning; the best known one has been published by J. Bowlby in his three volumes "Attachment and Loss". Bowlby distinguishes in his work four phases, each following the other: incredulity, with impulses of pain and intense anger; grieving and inner emptiness; despair, in the literal sense of the loss of hope to recover what has been lost; overcoming and reorganization. Each of these phases can have a different duration in time and sometimes the fourth and last phase is never reached.

But there is, more often than we believe, an additional emotional experience connected with mourning, which is guilt. In the psychotherapy of patients tormented, maybe for years, by an unelaborated mourning, we find out that the biggest obstacle they have to overcome is the belief of not having done all that was necessary to avoid or delay the loss of the loved one. The thought of not having called the ambulance or of having chosen the wrong doctor, or maybe of not having been present at the moment of the passing away because we were on vacation may never leave the mind of the person who has decided to define himself guilty. To leave an open account in the family ledger book, as resentments for unresolved discussions, will further complicate the process of elaboration and overcoming of the mourning. Furthermore, there's a particular and complicated case of loss situation that leads to develop a sense of guilt denominated "of the survivor". The best known example is relat-

173

ed, indeed, to the survivors of the Nazi concentration camps who had witnessed the extermination of many of their loved ones and often of their whole family. To realize of being the only individual still alive before such horror allowed and left a feeling of injustice for having been spared from death for no apparent reason if not for mere luck. Some of them committed suicide to stop the feeling of oppression by this "guilt". However, this guilt of the survivor can be perceived with great pain also by a parent who suffers the death of a child, or by a child in the case of a brother or sister's death.

In general, this feeling can affect whoever has to deal with situations of dramatic rupture of a strong emotional bond, experienced with an intense sense of injustice and absurdity for the event until then reputed to be inconceivable.

The detachment

"No one should notice you have lived."
(Epicuro, Scritti Morali)

"Acta est fabula, plaudite!"
"Applaud if you enjoyed the show!"
(Cesare Augusto)

The monk who at the end of the day knocked on the brothers' cells door who were getting ready to sleep, saying "Memento mori" (remember that you must die), highlighted effectively what distinguishes us from the other living beings, that is the awareness that we must die and the ability to share this thought with others. The anguish of death is so intense and pervasive that man has always tried to counteract and control it with every means. To believe that death represents only a moment of passage into another life, whether it is the Hades of the Greeks or the Elysian Fields of the Romans, or the garden of delights for Muslim males or the ecstatic contemplation of God for Catholics, or even the reincarnation into a new life for some eastern religions, is a very comforting and effective strategy for those who are facing the harsh reality of the annihilation of their existence.

The embalming, practiced in many cultures and not only by Egyptians, was another attempt, usually reserved for top-rank people, to try to deny the unavoidability of this event. Mausoleums, funereal monuments and all the other analogous majestic buildings that, with few exceptions, today often remain the only

175

still standing vestiges of ancient civilizations, were built to the same purpose. To deny the reality of our being *impermanent*, a word derived from Sanskrit and used by Buddhism, men have always wanted to leave on earth evidence of their passage by building something permanent like the pyramids.

So, the need for the sacred arises from this necessity to restrain the anguish of death through rituals of burial and the building of lasting funeral works in order to delude ourselves of making our brief existence less ephemeral. This need probably accompanies humans since even before the acquisition of the language, given that evidences of funeral rituals related to burials of Neanderthal men, who supposedly were still without a language and unable to articulate actual words, have been discovered and documented in different European localities, equipped with flowers and other simple objects.

From fossils and DNA analysis it seems that about 500,000 years ago this homo neanderthalensis separated himself from the same lineage from which the homo sapiens, with whom he shared more than 99,5 percent of genes, evolved, and has slowly colonized much of Europe and central Asia. He disappeared quite mysteriously about 30,000 years ago and many researchers argue on the hypothesis that it happened because of the evolutionarily losing competition with our species.

The unavoidability of death is therefore a common awareness that, until we feel good and able to conserve a satisfactory self-esteem, it remains in the

176

background for most of our existence, even if at any moment distressing emotions could emerge when an event is experienced as a serious and unavoidable threat to our security and emotional stability. As we have seen, this is the case of the loss of a loved one, of the house or in the case of an unexpected development of a serious illness. But it's only with the cognitive and emotional acquisition of knowledge of "being by now old", that the thought of having to die becomes a constant with which we deal daily.

So, the passage from adulthood to old age is characterized by the certainty of having by now reached the end of the life path and this universal theme has been depicted in various ways and in all cultures in religious iconography, in art and literature, as the skulls and the crossbones so widespread in Baroque churches, the hourglasses that are exhausting their last grains of sand or the symbolic references to the autumn leaves or the last lights of the day. In any case to be a senior and last stage of life, forces individual to acknowledge the rapid change which occurs rather in an underhand manner in the body, analogous and reversed to the one experienced many years before in the passage from childhood to adulthood. While the first change prepares the individual to fully face life by activating all his resources, the last one signals that we have to prepare ourselves to abandon our attachment to life and to detach from it definitively.

If all goes well and we succeed in avoiding as long as possible a disabling illnesses, keeping a decent clarity of mind and to be self-sufficient, we must in any case deal with the progressive decline of the psy-chophysical abilities, the loss up until the complete cessation of sexual desire and the slow but constant worsening of health status; all this will force us to deeply change our ways of relating with the world and to face the inevitable frustrations and the narcissistic wounds due to a state of growing social marginaliza-tion. Our current society based on personal success, competition and generalized access to information through the web has obsoleted the figure of the old man loaded with wisdom whom once was listened to, respected and protected, because he dispensed useful suggestions and wisdom to young people from his ex-perience of life. Nowadays, those who *appear* old are very often object of compassion, indifference or worse contempt. For this reason, many people tend to reject and deny as long as possible their state of oldness re-sorting to aesthetic operations and various drugs to maintain the appearance of a still relatively young and active person and to delay as long as possible the marginalization that usually, except in special cases, our culture reserves to old people.

Today old age and death, especially in big cities, are often accompanied by a collective feeling very similar to reserve and shame, that leads to lock the elderly up in isolated rest homes and to attribute the death of a close relative to a strictly personal event to the point of inducing the family in avoiding any public display of mourning. The tradition that, until a few decades ago, even in the big cities, entailed the pas-sage of the funeral procession through the whole town or district to the cemetery, with a carriage pompously adorned and pulled by horses, preceded by the band and followed by a long procession of people dressed in black, has been almost everywhere abandoned, just as the custom of wearing black clothing or of putting a black strip around the arm for a specified time, sometimes for a few years in sign of mourning. The ritual also entailed the intervention of specific brotherhoods, called Companies of the Good Death, that materially took care of organizing the funeral, by also supporting the family when needed, economically. Nowadays, we die in the hospital and no longer at home, and we move directly in dribs and drabs from the morgue to the cemetery, save for a brief stop in church for the farewell ritual. This leaves the family of the deceased emotionally alone and with more difficulties to manage, elaborate and overcome the highly dramatic event.

As at birth we begin to build our connections with the physical and relational world through systems of exploration and attachment, so the activation of these systems will cease at the end of our life, allowing us to detach ourselves more or less peacefully or painfully from everything that has defined and given meaning to our existence.

index